PLANNING IN YUGOSLAVIA

Organization and Implementation

by Albert Waterston

THE ECONOMIC DEVELOPMENT INSTITUTE

International Bank for
Reconstruction and Development

The Johns Hopkins Press,
Baltimore

© 1962 by The Johns Hopkins Press, Baltimore 18, Md.
Distributed in Great Britain by Oxford University Press, London
Printed in the United States of America by Garamond Press
Library of Congress Catalog Card No. 62-17544

Originally published, 1962
Second printing, 1966

FOREWORD

By the Director of the Economic Development Institute

THIS IS THE THIRD PUBLICATION of the Economic Development Institute. The Institute was established in 1955 by the International Bank for Reconstruction and Development. At the Institute, senior officials of member governments of the Bank are given an opportunity to study and discuss the practical problems facing them as administrators as well as the broad issues of economic growth and change which their preoccupation with day-to-day tasks often prevents their seeing clearly. An effort is made to put before them the growing experience of the Bank and of the international community as a whole in promoting economic development.

Publications of the Economic Development Institute are primarily designed for use by persons working in responsible administrative and advisory capacities in government, financial institutions or other important sectors of the economy of the Bank's less developed member countries. It is hoped that they may also prove informative and useful to educational institutions and groups and organizations of all kinds concerned with the problems of economic development.

The publications are the work of individuals. While in every case benefits have been derived from intimate contact with the work of the Bank, the publications in no sense purport to set forth the official views of the Bank or to be an authoritative statement of its policies in general or in detail.

John H. Adler

PREFACE

THERE ARE MANY STUDIES available which discuss techniques of planning but there are few which deal with the organizational and administrative aspects of planning or with the design of policies, procedures and institutional arrangements for implementing development plans. Because of the lack of published material in these fields, developing countries often establish their own machinery for planning and implementation without benefiting from the experience of other countries. As a consequence, they often spend undue amounts of time seeking solutions to problems and correcting errors which have been encountered before in other countries. These countries have, of course, used different methods to organize the preparation and execution of development plans and programs, with varying results. In spite of this diversity and of the political, economic and social differences among countries, which make it undesirable, even if it were possible, to evolve one planning system for all, there are nonetheless enough features common to most developing economies to make accounts of the experience of individual countries useful as guidelines for others.

For some years, the Economic Development Institute has been assembling, and using in its courses, documentation on the planning experience in developing countries. From these materials, several country case studies are being prepared. *Planning in Morocco* was the first and *Planning in Yugoslavia* is the second of these studies to be completed. Also under way is a comparative analytical study of planning experience in representative countries throughout the world, which will seek to draw such lessons and conclusions as may be useful.

The material for this study came from Yugoslav and other publications, both official and nonofficial, listed in the bibliography, from two visits to Yugoslavia which the author made in May 1959 and September 1961, and from numerous conversations with Yugoslavs and other who have firsthand knowledge of Yugoslavia and Yugoslav planning. The author owes his greatest debt, however, to colleagues in the World Bank. Their patient and sympathetic guidance was of inestimable value.

So many persons have contributed to this study and have read and commented on the several drafts through which it proceeded to its present form that much space would be required to list their names. All richly deserve the thanks which the author extends to them. In particular, Augustin Papic, Dragoslav Avramovic, Andrew M. Kamarck and Victor Wouters made many thoughtful contributions which improved the study in many ways. Cyril Davies and Cyril Martin added valuable suggestions to make the study more readable. If errors remain, however, the fault clearly lies with the author. Special appreciation is also due to Michael Hoffman, who not only suggested in the first place that the study be made, but also provided unfailing assistance during its preparation.

Albert Waterston

TABLE OF CONTENTS

ESSENTIAL STATISTICS

Area:
  In square kilometers: 255,804
  In square miles: 98,608

Population (1961): 18,512,805
  Density:
    Per square kilometer: 72.4
    Per square mile: 191
  Annual Rate of Increase:
    (1957-1960): 1.4%
    (Estimated for 1960-65): 1.2%

Literacy: 80%

Employment in Socialized Sector (as of March 31, 1958):
              Total: 2,405,919
                of which the percentage in
                    Manufacturing, mining and quarrying: 39
                    Agriculture and forestry: 10
                    Construction: 10
                    Commerce and catering: 8
                    Arts and crafts: 6
                    All other sectors: 27

Rate of Exchange:
  Official rate: 300 dinars=US$1.00
  Settlement rate since Jan. 1, 1961: 750 dinars=US$1.00

Net Product in 1960:
  Net social product*: 2,660 billion dinars
  Net national product*: 2,800-3,000 billion dinars
  Per capita: 151,000-162,000 dinars
  In US dollars (est.): $300-$325

  *See footnote 5 for explanation of the difference between social and national product.

I.

INTRODUCTION

AMONG THOSE UNDERDEVELOPED nations of the world which possess a sizable private sector and some semblance of a market economy, few can claim the degree of success achieved by Yugoslavia in carrying out economic development plans. From 1953 to 1956, Yugoslavia's national income grew by over 8 percent annually and between 1957 and 1960 by almost 13 percent each year. It was not always so. From 1947 until 1950 or 1951, when Yugoslavia under Russian influence sought to develop its economy by a system of state enterprise and strong centralized planning and control of every important detail of economic life, the results were far less spectacular. There can be no doubt that the low level of growth between 1948 and 1952—the national income rose by less than 2 percent annually—was largely due to the failure of the Soviet bloc to live up to its commitment to supply Yugoslavia with essential machinery, equipment and supplies, but most Yugoslavs also agree that the system of "administrative" or "centralized" planning which prevailed in Yugoslavia during the period also contributed to the poorer showing.

The break in relations between Yugoslavia and the Cominform countries in 1948 led eventually to a series of changes in the Yugoslav system which radically transformed the old system of centralized planning and control into a planned economy in which socialized enterprises, operating under "a system of workers' self-management," made significant decisions within the framework of a market economy. The transition from Soviet-type planning which began in 1952 (although some changes were introduced

1

earlier) to a unique form which blends elements found in market and planned economies with some found in neither was at first hesitant, but in the last few years it has gained increasing momentum.

Because of the pre-1948 orientation of the country, the low level of economic resources and the need to test the new institutions before letting go of the old, it is understandable that some central controls were retained, especially in the earlier years of the "new economic system"; but, in addition, innovations like economic incentives, competition in the market among socialized enterprises, and indirect monetary and fiscal instruments of policy were seeming anachronisms which required time to be reconciled with accepted doctrine. Once these techniques were accepted, however, as concessions which could be made, at least for a time, in order to improve economic performance without jeopardizing the goal of socialization, the way was open to the decentralized execution of Yugoslavia's development plans. If, in the process of advancing decentralization, Yugoslavia has not become skeptical of ideology, it has at least adopted a pragmatic approach which has permitted it to make effective use of its own experience, as well as of the experience of other countries, whatever their political or economic philosophy. As material resources increased and it became less risky to try new economic ideas, centralism gradually gave way to decentralized decision-making.

In principle, Yugoslav authorities have sought ways of stimulating initiative and output wherever possible, by introducing or adapting economic incentives instead of by central direction and control. If one solution proved unsatisfactory, it was quickly amended or replaced by another which promised to be more effective. Many of the measures used to attain objectives were (and in some cases continue to be) temporary, to be discarded when the goals they were designed to achieve had (or have) been met.

The last decade in Yugoslavia has therefore been a period of improvisation and experimentation which has led to the establishment of a complex, yet flexible, economic system. The spectacular reorientation of the economy from authoritarian control of enterprises to workers' management is justly considered by Yugoslav planners to present "a unique social laboratory, in which all sorts of economic and sociological hypotheses are being tested as a matter of daily practice."[1]

Although the main outlines of the new system are now clearly defined, the Yugoslavs do not yet consider it perfected. Further changes are being made, but the superiority of decentralized decision-making over centralized controls in achieving a viable economy, with one of the highest rates of growth in the world, has been demonstrated so clearly that recent changes in the system are almost all in the direction of further decentralization. There is little likelihood of a significant reversal of this trend in the foreseeable future.

Planning in Yugoslavia has evolved as an integral part of the political and economic systems of that country. More than in any other, a study of the planning machinery must include a review of the country's political and economic systems. In spite of the fact that planning in Yugoslavia is uniquely tied to its political economy, and could not possibly be transferred unchanged to any other country, there are nevertheless important lessons to be learned from the Yugoslav planning experience which make its study worthwhile.

There are, however, difficulties in making a study of Yugoslav planning. The first has to do with the difference between Marxian terminology as employed in Yugoslavia and the terminology of the West. Attempts may be made to explain the difference, as they are in the text, but it is perhaps unavoidable that some terms will remain at least partially obscure. Differences between terms like "state ownership" and "social ownership" or "doctrinaire" and "dogmatic," which in Yugoslavia are fraught with meaning, may seem like quibbling to some outsiders. Secondly, the Western reader will find it helpful to remember that in Yugoslavia there must always be an acceptable theoretical Marxian justification for any important proposal or action, and that the theoretical justification may not appear as important or as understandable to the outside

---

1. Horvat, Branko and Rascovic, Vlado. "Workers' Management in Yugoslavia: a Comment," *Journal of Political Economy* (Chicago), Vol. 67, No. 2, April 1959, p. 198.

observer as it is to the Yugoslav. Finally, as in other economic systems, there are often differences in Yugoslavia between theory and practice which defy easy categorization. While these problems may make it difficult for the Western reader to fully grasp the underlying rationale for the evolution and operation of the Yugoslav planning system, they do not present an insuperable obstacle to gaining an insight into its essential features and an appreciation of its remarkable accomplishments in the last decade.

II.

THE PERIOD OF ADMINISTRATIVE PLANNING

INSTITUTIONAL BACKGROUND

THE PEOPLE OF YUGOSLAVIA are mainly of Slavic origin, but history and geography have divided an originally homogeneous group into a multireligious, multilingual and multinational people with wide regional variations of economic and social development. Yugoslavs sometimes point out that Yugoslavia is one country, with two alphabets (Latin and Cyrillic), three religions (Serbian Orthodox, Roman Catholic and Moslem), four languages (Serbian, Croatian, Slovenian and Macedonian), five nationalities (Serbs, Croats, Slovenes, Macedonians and Montenegrins), six republics (Serbia, Croatia, Slovenia, Macedonia, Montenegro and Bosnia-Herzegovina) and seven surrounding nations (Austria, Hungary and Rumania on the north; Bulgaria on the east; Greece and Albania on the south and southwest; and Italy on the west). Although Yugoslavia is predominantly a country of peasant farmers (over 70 percent of the population was engaged in agriculture at the end of World War II and over 50 percent still are)] Slovenia and Croatia had pockets of industry before 1939 and Serbia had a prosperous agriculture, which raised the average economic position of these three areas well above that of the country's three others: Bosnia-Herzegovina, Macedonia and Montenegro.

Yugoslavia emerged from the Second World War as a federated socialist republic with a one-party government headed by the Communist leaders who had fought successfully to free the country

5

from enemy occupation. The 1946 Constitution, which adhered closely to the Soviet Constitution of 1936, established a government which, although a federation of six "people's republics" in form, was strongly centralized, politically and administratively. Within the People's Republic of Serbia are two autonomous areas with special status to take account of the different national and cultural compositions of their populations: the Autonomous Province of Vojvodina in northern Serbia and the Autonomous Kosovo-Metohija Region in southern Serbia. Each republic (except Montenegro) and each of the two autonomous regions has a number of districts composed of communes, which are in turn divided into settlements. Montenegro now has only communes and settlements.

The Constitution of 1946 described the legislature, the Federal People's Assembly, as the supreme governmental authority. The Assembly had two houses of equal rank: a Federal Council, whose members were elected by all citizens on a countrywide basis; and a Council of Nationalities, whose members were elected by citizens on a territorial basis to represent the interest of the republics and autonomous areas.

The most important unit of the Federal People's Assembly was the Presidium. It had important administrative, legislative and judicial functions, including the right to promulgate and interpret laws and to organize the state administration. It also served as the Assembly's steering committee and acted for the Assembly when it was not in session.

The highest executive and administrative authority was "the Federal Government," composed of a premier, vice-premiers and federal ministers appointed by the Federal People's Assembly and responsible to it. The Constitution empowered the Government to execute laws and economic plans enacted by the Assembly, to supervise the operation of state agencies and to conduct foreign relations.

The organs of the Government included ministries, commissions and committees. Two commissions, the Federal Planning Commission and the Federal Control Commission, each had the rank of a ministry. The Planning Commission prepared and coordinated national economic plans and the Control Commission directed the execution of the laws and orders of the Government. In fields which did not warrant the establishment of ministries or commissions, committees functioned.

Each republic and autonomous region had its own constitution, legislature and administrative organization patterned on the federal model, except that the legislature of each was unicameral, without a council of nationalities. At the district and communal levels, the organs of local government were the people's committees, each dominated by a powerful executive committee. In practice, republican and local governmental bodies were little more than media for carrying out directives of the federal authorities.

By the end of 1946, the Government had nationalized industrial, mining and quarrying enterprises employing over 80 percent of the workers in these fields, almost all wholesale trading concerns and all banks and transport companies. By the end of 1948, the Government had taken over the remaining private industrial concerns and 97 percent of the retailing establishments, leaving only most peasant farms, some small handicraft and commercial establishments and some fishing units in private hands. In most cases, the law permitted a private owner of agricultural land to hold up to 25 hectares (one hectare equals 2.47 acres). Land held above these limits, as well as land owned by enemy nationals, wartime collaborators with the enemy, absentee landlords and others was confiscated and either converted into state farms or collectives or distributed in small parcels to landless or other poor peasants and war veterans.

The authorities started a vigorous campaign to collectivize all peasant holdings into "producers' work cooperatives" but ran into passive resistance from the peasantry. In spite of this campaign, peasants outside the producers' work cooperatives still owned almost 94 percent of the total arable land in 1948. In 1949, the Government intensified its campaign and, in spite of continued opposition from the peasantry, managed to increase the number of producers' work cooperatives sevenfold. At the height of the collectivization movement in 1952, however, no more than 25 percent of Yugoslavia's arable land was held in producers' work cooperatives and state farms.

THE FEDERAL PLANNING COMMISSION

Yugoslavia spent the first year and a half after the end of World War II repairing the severe war damage to its economy. On May 25, 1946, before reconstruction had been completed, the Government introduced and the Assembly passed "The Law on the Federal Economic Plan and State Planning Bodies," which provided for the preparation of a federal economic plan, the reorganization of all federal and republican governmental staffs to assure that the plan would be carried out effectively and the setting up of a Federal Planning Commission. The Federal Planning Commission had a President and one or more Vice-Presidents. Its members were appointed by the Government on the recommendation of the President of the Planning Commission. A Federal Statistical Office was also established as an agency of the Planning Commission.

The Planning Commission soon became one of the most powerful organs of the Federal Government. It not only was responsible for preparing and controlling the execution of federal economic plans, but also had authority to coordinate all economic planning in the country. It had the right to require any federal, republican or local governmental agency, or any cooperative or enterprise to furnish it with information, to propose measures to the Government for insuring proper fulfillment of plans and, in urgent cases, to stop any action by a federal, republican or local governmental agency which conflicted with the federal plan.

Planning agencies were also created in republics, districts and in some communes. Each planning body in the hierarchy was responsible to the one above it. Thus, the planning unit of the commune was responsible to its district planning agency, which in turn took orders from its republican planning commission. The Federal Planning Commission was the supreme planning authority and the planning bodies of the republics and the local governments, as well as the planning units of the federal economic ministries, were required to carry out its regulations, directives and decrees. They had to submit their draft plans to the Federal Planning Commission for approval. The Commission was also authorized to place representatives in all other planning agencies as advisers and observers.

THE FIVE-YEAR PLAN FOR 1947-51

Immediately after its establishment, the Federal Planning Commission started preparing an economic development plan. The Commission requested each state enterprise and cooperative to furnish information on its productive capacity and ability to produce, its raw material requirements and other matters. On the basis of the data furnished, the Commission set production targets and estimated the amount of materials required by each enterprise and cooperative. Taking into account projects for new plants, the Commission next fixed physical production targets and equipment and materials requirements for each industry in each of the six republics and, finally, for the whole country.

After about a year's work, the Federal Planning Commission completed and made public a "Five-Year Plan for the Development of the National Economy," modeled on the Russian five-year plans. The Plan covered the period from January 1, 1947, to December 31, 1951. It was presented to the Federal People's Assembly on April 24, 1947, and after a few days' discussion was unanimously approved on April 28, 1947, and made retroactive to the first of the year. As passed by the Assembly, the Five-Year Plan had the force of law.

The grand objective of the Plan was nothing less than the conversion of a technologically backward, largely agrarian economy into an industrialized nation in five years. Simultaneously, it aimed to raise the economic and social levels of the country's less developed republics to those of the more advanced by allocating proportionally greater investments to the less developed than to the more developed areas of the country. The national income in 1951, the last year of the Plan, was expected to be about double the prewar level. The greatest increase was to be registered in industrial output, which would increase to almost five times the 1939 level. Agricultural production was also to rise, but the targets for this sector were much more modest than for industry. Although the rate of investment was to be much higher than ever before, consumption standards and social services were nevertheless to rise appreciably.

The Plan fixed extraordinarily detailed quantitative production targets for 1951 for about 600 groups of commodities for the country as a whole and for each of the six republics. The glass industry, for example, had targets for ordinary glass, optical glass, safety glass for autos, fire-proof glass, glass containers for medical use, and glass for electric bulbs. Targets were set for the output of a wide range of consumer goods, including soap, sets of furniture, boxes of matches, pairs of stockings, pairs of shoes with leather soles, pairs of rubber footwear and pairs of rubber footwear for peasants. The quantity of goods and the number of passengers to be carried, in 1951, by each mode of transport were enumerated. The number of telegrams to be sent and the number of telephone calls to be placed were estimated, as were the number of restaurants, the number of meals they would serve, and the estimated number of days which the estimated number of tourists would spend at the estimated number of hotels. For agriculture, the 1951 target for each agricultural commodity was specified, as was the number of fruit trees (divided by type: olive, plum, apple, etc.), areas of vineyards, number of each kind of livestock, amount of poultry, millions of eggs which hens would lay, milk yield per cow, kilograms of wool per sheep, etc., etc. (A more detailed description of the Plan is given in Appendix A.)

The Government was aware that the targets in the Plan were ambitious and that in seeking to industrialize a technically backward economy in five years it was setting its sights high. It was recognized that more skilled workers would be needed to achieve the targets and the Plan provided for training courses to increase the supply of semi-skilled and managerial personnel. Most of all, the Government expected that idealism and the internal cohesion of the population, which followed victory in World War II, would make workers approach the tasks laid down in the Plan with an uncommon will to work. The Five-Year Plan made it "the duty and privilege of every citizen" to carry out the Plan "with discipline and punctuality" and trade unions were encouraged to promote "socialist competition" among workers and factories to fulfill and exceed the targets in the Plan. By promoting competition, by singling out and rewarding those who were outstanding, by mechanization, rationalization and economies of scale, the Government believed that the country could fulfill or even exceed the Plan's targets.

FINANCING THE PLAN

During the period of "centralized planning," the federal budget was virtually the financial plan for the Yugoslav economy, controlling and disposing of two-thirds or more of the national income. It was the major source of investment funds for the Five-Year Plan. It not only handled receipts and expenditures of the Federal Government, but also the funds of the republican and local governments. The main source of revenue for the federal budget was the turnover (sales) tax in the socialized sector and the income tax in the private sector (levied mainly on farmers and artisans). As the chief fiscal instrument, it had the dual function of providing investment and other budgetary funds and restricting consumption by raising consumer prices.

Investment funds came largely from the federal budget, mainly in the form of grants; they were supplemented to some extent by profits of enterprises and short-term credits. Since the composition of production was determined administratively, these grants and bank credits did not appreciably influence output, nor was production greatly influenced by prices, which were used by the authorities as a tool of distribution.

The National Bank, Yugoslavia's central bank, was supposed to make cheap credit available to enterprises in amounts no more than needed to fulfill their production quotas. In practice, however, it granted an excessive quantity of credits, which helped bring on an inflation in which investment was partly financed through forced savings. Contributions from abroad also helped finance the investment program. UNRRA alone contributed about US$450 million of which US$145 million was in machinery and equipment. Reparation payments from former enemy countries added to investment funds as did, to a much smaller extent, commercial and public credits from Eastern Europe.

IMPLEMENTATION OF THE PLAN

The Five-Year Plan gave production targets only for 1951, the last year of the plan period. For each year in which the Plan was in effect, the Federal Planning Commission prepared, and the Federal Assembly approved, an annual plan, setting out the targets for the year. The Planning Commission then prepared a "basic plan" for each of the federal economic ministries which administered the targets. The combined "basic plans" included detailed production targets for about 2,000 groups of commodities. In cooperation with the Federal Planning Commission, the economic ministries then prepared even more detailed sets of targets, which were combined into a countrywide "operational plan" containing production targets for 16,000 to 20,000 commodities. Each ministry then assigned, usually through an intermediary organization known as a "directorate" or an "economic association" (of plants into which each branch of industry was organized), monthly production quotas and allocations of raw materials to each enterprise. Using these monthly plans as a basis, each enterprise then prepared 10-day and daily production and raw material consumption plans which it used to carry out its allotted task. Enterprises were also required to prepare daily work plans for every worker employed.

In agriculture, there were country, republican, district and communal sowing plans for crops, and plans for controlling the kind and quantity of animals raised. On the basis of these geographic plans and subplans, each state farm, producer work cooperative and private farm received targets, indicating the kind and amount of crops and animals it was expected to produce each year. A system of state purchase required compulsory deliveries of agricultural produce at low fixed prices. However, the Government relied heavily on an acceleration of collectivization to help bring about the fulfillment of the goals of the Five-Year Plan in agriculture.

Accordingly, regulations were adopted which favored cooperatives and state farms and discriminated against private farms. Tractors were to be made available only to producers' work cooperatives and state farms. Heavy taxes were levied on the land and income of private farmers and restrictions were placed on the number of laborers they could hire.

Each republic, district and commune also prepared annual and quarterly plans which were extensions of the federal annual plan. As in the case of the federal plans, approved republican plans and local plans acquired the force of law. The republican economic ministries supervised the execution of the plans by enterprises within their territory and were responsible to both the republican government and to the corresponding federal economic ministries. However, the instructions and regulations of the federal economic ministries took priority and, for all practical purposes, the planning and administration of investment was effectively centralized in the capital.

This was precisely the way the federal planners intended it to be. They strove unremittingly to consolidate the centralization of administrative authority, convinced that the more concentrated the controls, the more efficient and speedy would be the fulfillment of the plans. Agencies of the Federal Government not only prepared the plans but also controlled their execution. Each federal economic ministry concerned with a specific sector of the economy regulated all the important activities of the enterprises in its sector, either directly or indirectly, through a federal, republican or local authority reporting to the ministry. The ministry appointed the manager of the enterprise, who responded to the will of the distant ministry in Belgrade. It not only allocated raw materials and set production quotas for each enterprise, but prescribed the distribution of its output, the prices at which it was to be sold and the wages and working conditions of its workers. In the retrospective words of one high Yugoslav official: ". . . almost everything was planned from above, and the enterprise had nothing to plan."[2]

2. Boris Kidric in *BORBA,* August 26, 1951, as quoted by Alex N. Bragnich in: *Tito's Promised Land Yugoslavia.* New Brunswick, N.J., Rutgers University Press, 1954, p. 175.

THE PLAN'S DEFICIENCIES

Centralization of planning and execution and the subdivision of the federal annual plans into "basic" and "operational" plans, republican annual and quarterly plans, district and communal plans, and enterprise monthly, 10-day and daily plans, required a great deal of paper work and a large bureaucracy. It has been estimated that the completed annual plan weighed about 3,300 pounds![3] There were over 215 federal and republican ministers issuing orders for enterprises to carry out. The Federal Planning Commission had a staff of about 700 organized into four sections, one of the largest of which was concerned with controlling the execution of economic plans. This inspection staff operated more or less independently of the large staff of the Federal Control Commission, which also checked administrative efficiency. There were also control commissions in each of the six republics, and in each district and commune. For a time, there were also People's Inspectorates, composed of private citizens who zealously sought out failures, dishonesty or other shortcomings of enterprises. In addition, the press felt free to check enterprises on its own. Officials frequently intervened arbitrarily in the daily operations of enterprises. As the multiplication of rules made the economy progressively more difficult to manage from the center, production was often impeded when officials failed to issue instructions or to set targets, prices or wages on time.

The number of administrative personnel in enterprises expanded greatly. Each enterprise was required to prepare daily reports on its production, raw materials and fuel consumption, the number of workers employed, etc. These reports were submitted to the local government or to the appropriate "economic association," which telegraphed them to the supervising ministry in Belgrade at the end of each work day. The ministry would then consolidate the reports it received and report to the Federal Planning Commission. It has been estimated that under this centripetal system each enterprise had to submit each year to the authorities from 600 to 800 reports.[4]

3. Bicanic, Rudolf. "Economic Growth Under Centralized and Decentralized Planning: Jugoslavia—A Case Study," *Economic Development and Cultural Change* (Chicago), Vol. 6, No. 1, October 1957, p. 66.
4. *Ibid.*

Since it was considered more important for an enterprise to fulfill its target than to reduce costs, maximize profits, improve the quality of its product, or use capital assets efficiently and maintain them, managers sought to meet their quotas no matter what the cost. Centralized controls stifled individual and local initiative and encouraged irresponsibility in both managers and workers.

When the Federal Planning Commission had called upon enterprises in 1946 to furnish estimates of plant capacity, production capabilities, and raw material and fuel requirements, enterprise managers with more zeal than technical knowledge tended to overstate production potentials and to understate raw material and fuel requirements. These errors were compounded when the Planning Commission increased these production estimates, in the belief that even higher output could be achieved with centralized planning and controls. Even though Yugoslavia had large underdeveloped resources and great potentialities for expansion, it was probably too much to expect that the large number of projects incorporated in the Plan could be completed within a period of five years. The cost of projects was substantially underestimated, sometimes because of the planners' inexperience, sometimes because the size of projects was increased after they had been started and often because sponsors feared their projects would be disapproved if realistic estimates of their cost were submitted. Yugoslavia had little industry in 1946 and a large part of the labor force was composed of unskilled industrial workers and peasants, many of whom were uneducated. The planners underestimated the amount of time it would take to train the skilled workers, specialists, technicians and administrators needed to operate existing factories efficiently, let alone the additional plants which were to be constructed under the Five-Year Plan.

Federalism also introduced special problems. Since recipients of grants from the federal budget generally had no obligation to repay, there was a scramble among republican and local officials to obtain grants for the construction of plants in their areas. The Federal Government was subjected to pressure from all sides, which it did not always resist successfully, to finance projects which were often ill-conceived, poorly located or larger than optimum size. Even where projects were well planned, execution was often slow and expensive because of inexperience and absence of local responsibility.

It is beyond the scope of this study to analyze, in detail, all the factors within the Plan itself which limited the results obtained, but some of these need to be mentioned. In retrospect, it is clear that the planners underestimated the foreign exchange required to carry out the large-scale investment program in the Plan, even though they counted on obtaining sizable aid from Eastern Europe. They also overestimated their domestic resources and their ability to divert a large part of these resources to investments without undermining production incentives. The Plan set difficult goals: it proposed to export more raw materials while greatly increasing domestic requirements for these materials and it sought to raise investment to unprecedented levels while trying to improve greatly the standard of living. During the plan's implementation, the planners' preoccupation with the construction of new plants made them neglect problems which were impeding production in existing plants, with the result that output of consumer goods was curtailed. Perhaps the most glaring mistake, however, was the attempt to increase agricultural output with inordinately low investment and a poorly conceived agricultural policy based on enforced collectivization, low prices for the compulsory deliveries of agricultural produce and high prices for goods which farmers bought.

THE KEY INVESTMENT PROGRAM

It is therefore probable that the Five-Year Plan was too ambitious to be carried out successfully even if all had gone well and that inexperienced planners overestimated both the potentialities of the Yugoslav economy at the time and their ability to control every detail of the economy. If so, there is no way of telling now. It is certain, however, that the break in relations in June 1948, with the subsequent economic boycott of Yugoslavia by the Soviet bloc (when the Plan was only in its second year), greatly reduced the possibilities of fulfilling the Plan. It became necessary for Yugoslavia to reorient her export and import trade from East to West, and to make greatly increased defense expenditures, which reduced the resources available for investment. The Yugoslavs had counted on the USSR and other Eastern European countries to provide large long-term credits and industrial machinery and equipment to fulfill the industrial program in the Plan. When it became evident in the spring of 1949 that these countries had no intention of delivering what they had promised, the original investment planned for the year was reduced. Even so, Yugoslavia had to use up most of its foreign exchange and monetary reserves and go into debt to Western suppliers. Despite these difficulties, Yugoslav officials continued to hope that the Five-Year Plan could be completed as originally planned, but in December 1949, it was necessary for the Federal People's Assembly to extend the period of the Plan's execution for a year through 1952. In 1950, a severe drought forced the Government to replace the Five-Year Plan with a smaller Key Investment Program which, while including some new projects and retaining many of the uncompleted projects begun under the Five-Year Plan, eliminated many others.

In the Key Investment Program, investment was concentrated on projects, such as fuel, power and transport facilities, which would eliminate bottlenecks, yield substantial returns quickly, and help improve the balance of payments. The dispute with Yugoslavia's former allies had made the future too uncertain, however, and no time was set for the completion of the Key Projects Program. As a matter of fact, it was not until the latter part of 1956 that the Program was completed.

RESULTS OF THE FIVE-YEAR PLAN

Except for 1951, gross investment in fixed capital averaged about 28 percent of gross social product.[5] If rising defense expenditures

5. Gross social product, as calculated in Yugoslavia, includes production and services in industry, agriculture, forestry, construction, transport, commerce, catering, tourism and crafts. It does not include services of government, defense, health and welfare, insurance, and scientific, cultural, political and professional organizations. Consequently, Yugoslav social product is from 10 to 15 percent lower and national income is about 3 percent lower (and percentages based on

after 1948 are taken into account (as well as offsetting deficits in the balance of payments), total investment and defense expenditures between 1947 and 1951 approached 40 percent of gross social product. Investments were largely directed into industrialization (especially heavy and basic industry), to the neglect of transport, commerce and especially agriculture.

Between 1948 and 1952, national income increased at an average annual rate of only 1.9 percent. On a per capita basis, the average annual increase was much lower, about 0.4 percent. Although the physical volume of industrial production rose by 6.4 percent annually, and transport by 6.9 percent, agricultural output declined each year by 1.5 percent on the average and construction by 0.9 percent. Most of the growth in industrial output took place before 1950: by 1950 output had virtually ceased to expand, and in 1951, it declined.

Yugoslavs hold the view that, in spite of its shortcomings and the poor results obtained from the Five-Year Plan, centralized management of the economy in Yugoslavia was necessary immediately after the war to consolidate the newly nationalized economy, and that it served a useful purpose in the initial postwar planning period. On the other hand, they have frequently pointed to the serious weaknesses they discovered when planning was handled by a "central bureaucratic administrative apparatus." They recognized that "things went further in this direction than was necessary . . . [and that], during the few years of building socialism in Yugoslavia, the harmful effects of such a [centralized] system have been shown up. Wherever bureaucratic centralism appeared, it put a brake on initiative. Wherever inflexible, bureaucratic, centralistic planning reared its head, there was disorder in production and distribution."[6] With the authority that comes from experience, a

them are correspondingly higher), than gross national product and national income calculated by conventional western methods. In Yugoslav terminology, national income is gross social product less material expenditures and depreciation. In using or interpreting Yugoslav national accounts data, one must bear these differences in mind, as well as the fact that they are subject to fairly large price distortions among sectors.

6. Professor Leo Gerskovic, at the time Deputy Minister in the Council for Legislation of Development of People's Government, in: *Review of International Affairs* (Beograd), June 21, 1950, p. 20.

prominent Yugoslav economist has written eloquently of the self-defeating effects of centralization in breeding bureaucracy and inflexibility:

> To those who have lived under a system of centralized, bureaucratic, normative planning, its expense in human and economic terms and the damage which it can do at all levels of the economy are obvious. Sometimes people, particularly economists, are led astray by the bias for rationalization to the superficial assumption that centralization means greater efficiency and greater speed. The balancing of supply and demand in a centrally planned economy occurs in offices where a few people, unaware of the real effects of their authoritarian plans, become the supreme judges of the destinies of all producers and consumers through their bureaucratic machine. From this source of authority plans lead further down to smaller bodies, splitting unrealistic averages into still smaller averages, according to norms born in offices which, when they reach the enterprise level, have little resemblance to the conditions of actual life.[7]

7. Bicanic, "Economic Growth Under Centralized and Decentralized Planning: Yugoslavia—A Case Study," p. 66.

III.

DECENTRALIZED PLANNING: SOCIAL, ECONOMIC AND POLITICAL CHANGES

WHEN IT BECAME APPARENT in the latter part of 1949 that the split with the Cominform countries was likely to endure, there began in Yugoslavia a period of intensive questioning and criticism of formerly sacrosanct doctrines and policies and a search for another course toward socialism which did not have the disadvantages of Soviet-type centralized planning and controls. This led, from 1950 through 1952, to a series of fundamental policy reformulations and to a longer period of experimentalism, often notably free of dogmatism,[8] from which there gradually evolved, by trial and error, a new structure of political and economic relationships which reversed the trend toward centralization.

Although the dispute between Yugoslavia and the Soviet bloc had deeper roots, it was generally couched in ideological terms. One of the charges which the USSR had levied against the Yugoslavs was that they were moving too slowly toward nationalizing the economy, particularly agriculture. Although they, at first, sought to meet this criticism by stepping up collectivization, the Yugoslavs eventually took the position that, far from being too slow, they might have gone too far in following the Soviet system

8. Thus, Tito was reported to have said, "For us the collective farms are not a matter of dogma. We are not concerned about the forms—about whether they are called socialist or not. What we need is more agricultural production—more bread. We are trying to find means of getting it." in "Interview with Marshal Tito, President of Yugoslavia, *U.S. News and World Report,* Vol. 34, No. 16, April 17, 1953, p. 26.

where, they said, substitution of the state for private owners had not materially improved the position of workers and employees. Yugoslav theorists advanced the view that state ownership and management of enterprise led inevitably to regimentation and wasteful bureaucratic centralism. They took the position, moreover, that conditions had now been established in their country which would permit an acceleration of the process by which a socialist state gave way to "society" through a "withering away of the state." It is this concept which underlay the economic, social and political reforms introduced after 1949.

"SOCIAL OWNERSHIP"
AND "WORKERS' SELF-MANAGEMENT"

As a first step toward bringing about a "withering away of the state," laws were enacted as early as 1950 which formally transferred ownership of state enterprises to "society" and vested control over the operations of each "socially-owned" enterprise in its workers to administer as trustees of society. This distinction between governmental administration and the administration of enterprises, i.e., the management of "socially-owned property" by the workers instead of by the state, has been described by some Western observers as "pseudo-decentralization" and mere window-dressing to conceal actual state ownership and operation by the Russians as "the blossoming of private enterprise" and by the Yugoslavs as "a higher form of socialist ownership."

Under the new system of self-management, which is the keystone of the new system, the workers in each enterprise elect biannually a "workers' council" to which they delegate general responsibility for the operation of the enterprise. The workers' council examines and approves the firm's annual economic plan, contracts investment loans, approves the enterprise's balance sheet and, most important of all, disposes of the enterprise's profits. The members of the workers' council elect, from their own ranks, 3 to 11 members to constitute a "management board," which assists the manager, an *ex officio* member of the board, in running the enterprise. The manager, who is selected by public competition by the workers' council with the approval of the local council of producers (one of the two houses of the commune's legislative body), directs the day-to-day activities of the enterprise, subject to review by the management board. While the extent to which workers, their workers' council or management board actually participate in management varies from enterprise to enterprise, observers agree that, in general, workers' self-management has increased the influence of workers in the management of enterprises.

Most administrative controls on enterprises have been eliminated and they now have much greater operational autonomy and initiative than in the previous period. Each enterprise is now generally free to determine what it will make, where it will buy, to whom it will sell, what prices it will charge, what to import and export, how much its workers earn and how much it will invest.

Unlike the situation which prevailed during the period of centralized planning, when workers and managers were paid whether or not their enterprise was profitable, the incomes of both workers and management now largely depend on the earnings of their enterprise. The greater the earnings, the more they receive. Enterprises, therefore, have a much stronger incentive than hitherto to cut costs and increase sales. Moreover, in order to retain its autonomy, an enterprise must be run in a businesslike way. The test of its efficiency is its ability to compete in the market. If it runs at a loss, an official receiver may replace the workers' council and it may be forced into bankruptcy and reorganized. Plant, equipment and raw materials are no longer furnished without charge. As indicated in greater detail in a later section, each enterprise must defray out of its total receipts a depreciation allowance on its fixed assets, the cost of materials and services it uses in production, interest on investment and short-term credits, and a variety of taxes, before the workers' council is allowed to allocate the balance, either to wages and salaries or to the enterprise's reserve, investment or social welfare funds.

The principle of self-management has been widely applied outside industry. As the planners point out, "Factories with workers' management are just one link in the chain (and) . . . it would be very misleading to regard workers' management as a sort of *deus ex machina* in an otherwise familiar scene. . . . The basic feature of the new scene consists in the idea of self-government in every sphere of social and political life. Society is conceived as a federation of self-governing and interconnected association."[9] Workers' management exists in wholesale and retail establishments, agricultural cooperatives, foreign trade and transport enterprises and public utilities as well as in industry. The principle of self-management is also applied to housing cooperatives, universities and other schools, hospitals and other social service institutions, scientific and other professional organizations and railways, post offices and other service organizations.

REFORMS IN AGRICULTURE

The decentralization movement also affected agriculture, but fundamental changes in this sector did not come until 1953. Sowing plans were abandoned, compulsory deliveries at artificially low prices were abolished, discriminatory income taxes were replaced by taxes, based on a reasonable cadastral valuation of land, which provided farmers with economic incentives to increase output. Peasants were encouraged to plant the most profitable crops and to sell their produce on the free market or at guaranteed prices, whichever was higher. When, beginning in 1953, they were permitted to leave the producers' work cooperatives, there was a wholesale exodus which left only about 6 percent of the country's cultivated land in producer work cooperatives and 3 percent in state farms.

At the same time, however, the maximum amount of arable land which a private holder could normally retain was again reduced, this time to 10 hectares (25 acres). The authorities announced that it remained their long-term goal to collectivize agriculture, but by means of persuasion instead of coercion. For the time being, however, the government recognized that it was more important

9. Horvat and Rascovic. "Workers' Management in Yugoslavia—a Comment," p. 197.

that agricultural output be increased than that land be nationalized. Expansion of the socialized sector was to be accomplished gradually by the purchase of land from the increasing number of peasants who left their farms to take jobs in the expanding industrial sector, as well as through land reclamation, renting from owners and by making it attractive to peasants to join voluntary cooperatives of which the general cooperative is the most popular type. Members of general cooperatives, as distinguished from the old producers' work cooperatives, retain ownership of their land, have a great degree of freedom in managing their cooperatives and have the right to leave the cooperative after the termination of their contract.

In order to induce peasants to join the general cooperatives, which are in any case attractive to them since they provide a variety of production, processing, marketing, purchasing, sales and other services farmers need, the authorities channel through the cooperatives most investment and other credits for agriculture, subsidized fertilizers, fuel, machinery, improved seeds, breeding stock and extension services. Private peasants may operate their farms, buy materials and sell their produce as they wish, but since efficient farming of small parcels of land is difficult without the aids available to members of the general cooperatives, they have attracted an increasing number of members. Although cooperatives and state farms together account for only about 8 percent of holdings of cultivated land, the holdings of the cooperatives average 350 hectares (875 acres) and those of the state farms 900 hectares (2,250 acres) while the average holding of the 2.5 million private farmers is only 4.6 hectares (11.5 acres). The cooperatives and state farms have, therefore, found it much easier to apply efficient methods to their larger holdings than have the small private farmers and have led in improving production and marketing techniques and in increasing output. As a result, yield per hectare on state farms as well as on cooperative lands is appreciably greater and in some cases double that of private farms.

CHANGES IN POLITICAL ORGANIZATION AND FUNCTION

The introduction of workers' management not only required fundamental modifications of the economic system but also made necessary a drastic reorganization of government administration and a significant reduction in the size of the state apparatus dealing with economic affairs. After a series of more or less makeshift interim changes, which attempted to keep governmental machinery reasonably abreast of the many changes in the economy, the Federal People's Assembly completely revised the structure of government on January 13, 1953, by amending the 1946 Constitution. The Presidium, the Federal Government, the ministries and the Federal Control Commission were abolished. The principle of "government by assembly" was, however, reaffirmed, with the Federal People's Assembly as the highest organ of authority of the Federated People's Republic of Yugoslavia.

While the new Federal People's Assembly is, like its predecessor, bicameral, it is now composed of a reconstituted Federal Council and a brand new Federal Council of Producers. (See chart on next page.) In economic matters, including approval of development plans, the Federal Council and the Federal Council of Producers are on an equal footing and the consent of both is needed for passage of legislation. Each house of the Federal People's Assembly has its own working committees, where much of the basic work on pending legislation takes place. For the purpose of the development plans, the separate Committees for National Economy of the Federal Council and of the Council of Producers are the most important.

The two houses of the Federal People's Assembly jointly elect from their membership the President of the Republic and from the membership of the Federal Council, a Federal Executive Council. The President of the Republic and the Federal Executive Council are the executive arms of the Federal People's Assembly and are constitutionally responsible to it. The President of the Republic is endowed with great powers, both as Head of State and as *ex officio* President of the Federal Executive Council. The Federal Executive Council has extremely broad powers. It not only enforces all

THE FEDERAL PEOPLE'S ASSEMBLY AND ITS EXECUTIVE ORGANS

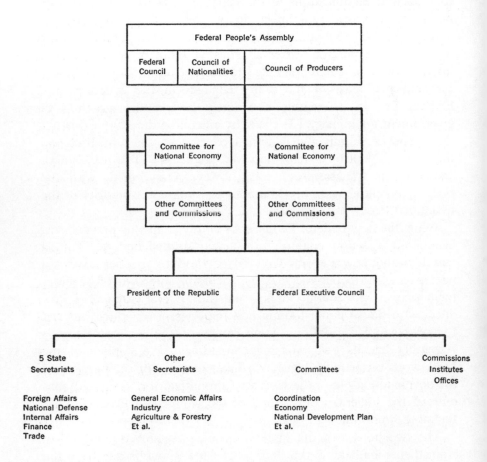

Source: Adapted from the Statistical Pocket Book of Yugoslavia, Federal Statistical Institute, Beograd, April 1961, p. 161

federal laws, appoints and dismisses all high officials of the Federation and supervises the operation of its executive branch, but also initiates and presents federal development plans and budgets to the Federal People's Assembly.

There are a series of state and other secretariats, committees, commissions, institutes and offices which operate under the direct jurisdiction and policy direction of the Federal Executive Council. Their most important task is to issue rules, orders and instructions to implement and enforce decisions and other acts of the Federal Executive Council. The Federal Institute of Economic Planning and the Federal Statistical Institute (which together replaced the old Federal Planning Commission) also report to the Federal Executive Council. The Coordination Committee and two other committees of the Federal Executive Council, the Committee of the National Development Plan and the Committee of the National Economy, play important roles in the preparation of Yugoslavia's development plans.

The six republics and the two autonomous areas have governmental systems which are essentially like those of the Federation. Each republic and the Autonomous Province of Vojvodina has its own bicameral assembly, composed of a council and a council of producers, and an executive council elected by its assembly. The Autonomous Kosovo-Metohija Region, the districts and the communes each has a bicameral legislative body called a "people's committee," also composed of a council and a council of producers, as well as an executive council modeled on the federal pattern.

The structure of the bicameral people's committee in the local governments, especially the commune's, has been devised to reflect the political and economic interests of the local citizens. The Yugoslavs attribute special importance to the fact that the "direct producers" in economic organizations (a generic term which includes economic enterprises, associations of economic enterprises and farm, handicraft, trade, consumers and certain housing cooperatives) in each locality elect representatives, on the basis of occupation, to the producers' council of each people's committee. The people's committees of the local governments are linked to the Federal People's Assembly through the constitutional provision that deputies of the Federal People's Assembly are *ex officio* members of the legislative bodies of the localities from which they were elected.

DEVOLUTION OF FEDERAL FUNCTIONS

In the process of reorganization, the Federation transferred most of the functions, formerly exercised by its own civil service, either to elected members of the Federal People's Assembly, but more often to elected officials of the republics and local governments. As a result, the republics and local governments acquired substantial powers which formerly had been the exclusive prerogative of the federal "bureaucracy." The Federation drastically reduced the size of its civil service (the number of those on the federal payroll declined from 43,500 in 1948 to 8,000 in 1955). In fact, the reduction in federal employees may have gone too far, for since 1958 there has been some increase in the number. Many federal employees who had formerly worked in enterprises returned to them. Opportunities were also offered to displaced employees to work at the republic and local levels, if they were qualified or took the necessary technical training to qualify for positions in republican or local administrations. At the same time, local governmental administrations were also reorganized to put them in a better position to handle their new responsibilities.

The "self-governing autonomous commune," which in rudimentary form dated from the early years of World War II, was elevated after 1950 to the position of the basic unit of political, social and economic control. In the Yugoslav *milieu,* the commune occupies a unique place as one of the pillars of the new social and economic order. It is considered both a governmental and non-governmental form, "a symbiosis of local self-government and the machinery for social management concretized at the level of the local community."[10] Since 1955, the number of functions (especially in the economic field) assigned to communal people's committees has

10. Djordjevic, Jovan. "The Communal System in Yugoslavia," in "Collective Economy in Yugoslavia," *Annals of Collective Economy; International Review* (Geneva), Vol. 30, No. 2/3, April/November 1959, p. 170.

trebled, while those of the republics and the districts have been progressively reduced. The commune has thus acquired great powers. A new constitution, to be promulgated in 1962, is expected to extend the power of communes further. By making most of the commune's revenues dependent on the levels of income of individuals and economic organizations in its area, the commune's local pride has been reinforced with economic incentives to promote the economic development of its territory. Besides receiving a share of the proceeds of some federal taxes, communes have authority to impose their own taxes and exercise a large measure of control over their own budgets and investment funds.

The commune is one of the important means by which social control is exercised over local social and economic activities. It has supervisory authority over hospitals, schools, housing units, agricultural and artisan cooperatives, and public services, each of which is, however, endowed with varying measures of autonomy. It also supervises enterprises and other economic undertakings in its territory to assure that their responsibilities, as determined by appropriate laws, are fulfilled. (As will be explained later, except for defense enterprises, railways and electric power companies in regional or national grids, no enterprise is now under direct federal or republic control.) The commune participates in the appointment of the managing directors of economic organizations, checks on the legality of enterprise decisions, inspects their financial management and has the right to object to their wage and salary scales. It establishes new undertakings and promotes their development and it gives its guarantee when enterprises contract with banks for investment and other credits. While the commune therefore exercises a considerable influence over economic organizations, "it has no right to intervene in the organization of economic and working processes, or in the economic operation and administration of undertakings."[11]

If the commune is powerful, it is also subject to the control of those controlled with the result that it is sometimes uncertain whether economic organizations have more influence on the communes or *vice versa*. Since the council of producers of the

11. *Ibid.*, p. 194.

commune's people's committee is composed of workers and employees from the economic organizations in its territory, as well as trade unionists, artisans and farmers, Yugoslav planners contend that "when the 'local authority' through the council of producers interferes with the affairs of a *particular* factory, it is a very special kind of interference."[12]

12. Horvat and Rascovic. "Workers' Management in Yugoslavia: a Comment," p. 197.

IV.

DECENTRALIZED PLANNING: ORGANIZATION OF PLANNING

PLANNING OFFICES

As THE DECENTRALIZATION movement gained momentum after 1952, the Federal Planning Commission was progressively stripped of its executive and administrative powers over the economy to bring it into line with the diminishing role of the Federal Government in implementing economic plans. As an indication of its changing status, the name of the Federal Planning Commission was transitionally changed to the Federal Chief Administration for Planning and, in 1953, to the Federal Institute of Economic Planning (referred to hereafter as the Federal Planning Institute). At the same time, the statistical section of the Federal Planning Commission was set up as an independent Federal Statistical Institute. The number of people employed by the Planning Commission declined from about 700 to about 50 at the low point.

While the Federal Planning Institute is responsible for drafting all federal "social" plans (as all Yugoslav governmental development plans are called), it is far less powerful than its original predecessor, the Federal Planning Commission. The powers of the Federal Planning Institute are only technical and advisory and it has no executive authority over the operation of the economy. Beyond the drafting of plans for submission to the Federal Executive Council and the Federal People's Assembly, its field of action is limited to analyzing the extent to which the plans have accomplished what they set out to do, studying potentialities for further development, evolving appropriate planning methods and techniques and recommending the "economic instruments" or measures by which the social plans are implemented.

Responsibility for reporting on the progress of execution of the *annual* plans rests with one of the secretariats of the Federal Executive Council, the Secretariat of Economic Affairs. The Secretariat prepares monthly progress reports and carries out such actions as the Federal Executive Council considers necessary to implement the plans. A few years ago, an attempt was made to limit the Federal Planning Institute to the planning of development plans of more than one year and to turn over the preparation, as well as reporting the progress of the yearly plans through which the longer-term plans are implemented, to the Secretariat of Economic Affairs. The move was supported by the argument that the annual plan was merely a device for carrying out the longer-term plans and not an integral part of these plans. Luckily, this attempt to divide the planning function was never carried out and the Secretariat remains concerned today only with reporting on the implementation of the annual plans, while the Federal Planning Institute retains the task of preparing all federal plans.

Economic planning offices similar to the Federal Planning Institute also replaced the former administrative-type planning organizations in the republics, the autonomous regions, the districts and the more advanced communes. Each planning agency is independent of any other planning agency and is directly responsible for its activities only to its own legislative body or executive council. No planning agency from the Federal Planning Institute down, now has the right to issue orders to another, "since this would run contrary to the social and economic order in Yugoslavia, especially to the principle of social [self] management."[13] The internal organization of each planning office depends on the governmental level on which it operates, the size, and degree of development of the territory for which it drafts plans and the complexity of the economic problems with which it deals.

The Federal Planning Institute is headed by a Director, assisted by two Deputy Directors. Unlike the situation during the period of

13. Kubovic, Branko, et alii. *Economic Planning in Yugoslavia.* Beograd, Jugoslavija, 1959, p. 50.

centralized planning when the heads of the Planning Commission were political officials, the Director of the Federal Planning Institute, his Deputies and the staff are mostly economists and other technicians selected on the basis of their qualifications. While the two Deputies may, on occasion, participate in all activities of the Planning Institute, one generally devotes himself to the preparation of the annual plans while the other concerns himself with the longer-term plans.

The Planning Institute has a staff of some 180 persons, less than one-third the number formerly employed by the former Federal Planning Commission. About half have university degrees. Some 40 members of the staff are economists, about 20 include lawyers, engineers, agronomists and forestry experts, chemists, geologists and other specialists, and the remaining 60 are high school graduates performing a variety of clerical and nonprofessional tasks (Appendix B gives the organization of the Federal Planning Institute).

The Planning Institute also maintains a committee of experts. Its regular members include the Director and his two Deputies and the heads of all the technical divisions of the Institute. When appropriate, the committee is enlarged by the inclusion of prominent outside economists and the directors of the republican planning offices. The committee meets from time to time, as necessary and especially just before the drafting of the federal plans, to discuss problems of methodology and development.

The republican planning offices have functions similar to those of the Federal Planning Institute, but their work load is, of course, much smaller, particularly in the field of international trade. Because their staffs are small, it is difficult for them to carry out systematic institutional research. The average republican planning office is likely to have the following seven sections: research, regional development, industry and mining, agriculture and forestry, investment and construction, other economic activities, and administration. Each republican planning office employs from 30 to 70 persons, the number generally being several times smaller than the republican planning commissions employed in the period of centralized planning. Like the Federal Planning Institute, republican planning offices also use panels or committees of experts.

District planning offices generally employ from 5 to 10 persons to carry out functions which are considerably narrower in scope than those of the republican planning bodies. They may have research and investment sections, but for the rest of their work they are likely to have one technician in charge of several activities in the district (e.g., transport, construction, trade, tourism and handicrafts). The planning units in the communes are usually even smaller than those in the districts, with the organization in each case adapted to the needs of the particular commune.

Various secretariats, offices, bureaus and other agencies of the federal, republican, district and communal administrations, as well as economic organizations and associations and chambers of enterprises or collectives, also have their own planning units which prepare projects, programs or other studies within the fields of their competence. They are important for economic planning, because they furnish basic information to the various governmental planning offices when the latter are drafting their plans.

At the federal level, the Federal Planning Institute maintains continuous contact and, in the course of preparing the federal plan, cooperates closely on an equal basis with federal secretariats and other federal agencies. This is in marked contrast to the situation during the period of centralized planning when the Planning Commission was on a higher level than the ministries. Because the various federal bodies follow economic developments, including implementation of the federal plans, in their respective fields of activity, they are able to make useful comments on the draft federal plans prepared by the Federal Planning Institute, prepare their own proposals and analyses or suggest economic measures for inclusion in the federal plans.

The Planning Institute's principal sources of information for preparing the federal plans are the Federal Statistical Institute, the National (central) Bank and the Investment Bank. These institutions provide regular statistical services and also carry out special inquiries during the preparatory phase of the plan. Because of the importance of the financial aspects of planning, cooperation between the Federal Planning Institute and the State Secretariat of Finance is also especially close and regular.

In preparing its plans, the Planning Institute prefers to rely on data furnished by the Federal Statistical Institute, the National Bank, the Investment Bank and other federal bodies to determine the investment and other economic roles of republics, local governments and economic organizations. The lack of direct information on enterprise intentions may appear to be a handicap,[14] but the Federal Planning Institute has felt no need as yet to collect such information and on the basis of results it seems to be right, at least until now.

Cooperation between the Federal Planning Institute and republican planning offices which, in turn, work closely with district and communal planning offices, manifests itself in many ways and especially in the preparation of draft social plans. Specifically, the Federal Planning Institute and each republican planning office work together in allocating available investment and other funds for underdeveloped regions in the republics, in defining the production and investment policies to be included in the republican plan and in prescribing measures in the republican plan for directing the economic development of an underdeveloped region, or an urban or industrial area in a republic. They also cooperate in devising uniform planning methods and organizational structures in planning offices at all levels, in order to ensure appropriate coverage of all important planning problems.

The various chambers of commerce and industry, economic associations and trade unions also have an important part in the preparation and execution of the governmental plans. These groups have much to say in the preparation and implementation of enterprise plans, as well as in the implementation of official economic policy. They form important links between the planning offices at all governmental levels and the economic organizations by

14. A group of UN observers thought that "now that enterprises have so much more freedom than before to allocate profits, at least some kind of sample inquiry—into investment intentions for example—would seem to be a useful tool for the planners to develop in future." in "Economic Planning and Management in Yugoslavia," *United Nations Economic Bulletin for Europe,* Vol. 10, No. 3, 1958, p. 45.

coordinating the plans of the groups of enterprises with which they work. There is also a variety of economic and technical institutes, which assist in the preparation of enterprise plans by preparing special studies on methods and economic problems.

DRAFTING THE PLANS

The Soviet-type planning methods used by the Federal Planning Commission during the period of centralized planning have either been discarded or greatly revised. The Federal Planning Institute now relies generally on an eclectic system of planning by a "system of balances," which includes refined econometric techniques familiar in western countries. The results obtained are then modified to some extent by common sense, political considerations and, in the interest of conservatism, by a bias toward understating potentialities for further growth.

The actual drafting of the plan goes through six interrelated stages:

1. The Planning Institute prepares a detailed analysis of the economic situation with special reference to possibilities for further growth.

2. On the basis of this analysis, the Federal Executive Council and the Federal People's Assembly define the general objectives of the plan.

3. On the basis of items (1) and (2), estimates of the possible development of production, national income, investment and personal income are made.

4. Partial plans for particular branches and sectors of the economy are then drafted (e.g., for industry, agriculture, capital investments, personal consumption). At this stage several variants are prepared to indicate alternative possibilities.

5. The most favorable variants and alternatives in the sector plans which are consistent with fixed objectives are next selected, coordinated and linked together into a comprehensive summary plan for the entire economy.

6. In the final drafting stage of the annual (but not in the multi-annual) federal plans, the economic measures by which the plan is to be implemented are formulated.

ADOPTION OF THE PLANS

When the preliminary draft federal plan is ready, generally at the beginning of October before the start of the plan period, the Federal Planning Institute submits it to the Federal Executive Council's Committee for the Economy,[15] if the plan is for one year, or to the Federal Executive Council's Committee for the National Development Plan,[16] if it is for a longer period. In actual practice, the Federal Planning Institute maintains constant contact with the appropriate Committee during the preparation of the federal plan. It is likely, therefore, to submit sections of the plan to the Committee even before the whole draft is completed. On the basis of the discussions in the appropriate Committee, the Planning Institute may be, and usually is, required to make changes in the draft plan. When the plan meets with the approval of the appropriate Committee, it goes to the Federal Executive Council for further examination. If the Federal Executive Council suggests changes, the plan is returned to the proper Committee or to the Planning Institute for modification.

When the plan is approved by the Federal Executive Council, generally by about the middle of October prior to the beginning of the next plan period, copies are forwarded to the Committees of the National Economy of the Federal Council and the Council of Producers of the Federal People's Assembly, where the draft plans are discussed independently by each Committee. A representative of the Federal Executive Council, who is empowered to make changes suggested by these Committees, provided they are not inconsistent with the basic objectives and scope set for the plan, sits

15. The members of this Committee include representatives from the Federal Executive Council, the corresponding committees for the economy of the various republics, the trade unions and the army.

16. The members of this Committee include representatives of the Federal Executive Council, the executive councils of all the republics, the trade unions, and the army.

with each Committee of National Economy during its deliberations. In theory, the Federal Executive Council would have to defend before each house of the Assembly a refusal to comply with a Committee's request for a change in the draft plan; in practice, agreement has always been possible at the Committee level and it has not been necessary to carry differences to the Assembly itself. When each Committee has concluded its deliberations, it presents a report to its legislative house, which may, and usually does, suggest amendments to the draft plan. Since in the Yugoslav system the federal plan embodies the government's economic policy, it holds the place that the budget normally occupies in most other countries and is debated accordingly in the Federal People's Assembly. After the plan has been discussed and passed in separate sittings of both houses (usually before the end of the year preceding the beginning of the plan period), it is published as an act of the Federal People's Assembly with the force of law. At the end of each plan period, the Federation must submit an audited report to the Federal People's Assembly, setting forth the manner and extent to which the plan for the period has been fulfilled.

Except for the Five-Year Federal Social Plan for 1957-61, when the Planning Institute submitted a first draft to a specially constituted advisory committee of economists, no formal procedure exists for discussion of draft federal plans outside official circles. However, even while the Federal Planning Institute is working on the draft plan, public discussion of its objectives begins in the press and in meetings of various economic and technical organizations. When the Federal Executive Council transmits the draft plan to the Committee of National Economy of the Federal Assembly, discussion of the plan in the press, technical periodicals and scientific and economic organizations proceeds apace. This early dissemination and widespread discussion of the draft plan have the advantage of contributing greatly to public understanding of the aims and contents of the plan and thereby facilitate more effective execution.

V.

DECENTRALIZED PLANNING: TYPES OF PLANS

ROLE OF THE FEDERAL PLANS

YUGOSLAVIA NOW REJECTS the theory which prevails in the Soviet Union and in other Eastern European countries that control of the economy through centrally directed measures constitutes the "fundamental law of socialism." Yugoslav planners now hold that "a central economic plan can never forecast all the details and complicated mutual relations of the entire process of production, the use of all producing capacities and reserves, the needs of consumption, etc."[17] For this reason, and because of the desirability of encouraging initiative on the part of producers and economic organizations, the federal plan no longer lays down production quotas for enterprises. This does not mean however, contend the planners, that the federal plan has become only a hypothesis of the future development of the economy, for the over-all production targets for the economy, as shown in the federal plan, are still considered obligatory and legally binding. Nevertheless, the practical significance of this position is hard to understand, since no person or enterprise is held legally accountable for fulfilling any target of the federal plans.

In theory, the federal plan remains the medium through which the state fixes the distribution of the national income, apportions national resources between savings and consumption, determines the rate of investment and its sectoral and, for underdeveloped

17. Kubovic, Branko, et alii. *Economic Planning in Yugoslavia,* p. 22.

regions, its geographical distribution. The first paragraph of Article 17 of the Constitution provides that "The Federal Social Plan ensures the development of the national economy as a whole and regulates the basic distribution of national income of the Federal People's Republic of Yugoslavia." Articles 1 and 2 of "The Law on Planned Management of the National Economy" of 1951 spell this idea out. "The management of the national economy shall be carried on pursuant to the social plan of the Federal People's Republic of Yugoslavia, the social plans of the People's Republics, autonomous regions, districts and communes and the independent plan of economic organizations. By setting basic proportions of production and distribution, social plans shall determine the direction of development of material productive forces and regulate the basic distribution of the national income among the consumption fund of working people, capital formation and other general requirements of the social community." This is the theory; in practice, however, the growing importance of the market has progressively converted the federal plan into a forecast based on certain investment and other assumptions. As a result, the federal plan, although still important as a force for development, plays a lesser role than formerly. It has become only one of several means of furthering governmental objectives.

REPUBLICAN, REGIONAL AND LOCAL PLANS

Every governmental unit concerned with management of the economy in Yugoslavia has "the right and duty" to draw up its own social plans. Accordingly, every republic, autonomous region, district and commune has its own plan. There are, however, two compelling reasons besides "right and duty" why economic planning below the Federation level is important in Yugoslavia. Each republic and locality has its special problems (e.g., low income or lagging social services) which demand special treatment. These local problems are not taken adequately into account in the federal plan. Even more important is the fact that implementation of the federal plan is largely decentralized in the republics and the localities.

If the federal plan is to be fulfilled, therefore, much time and attention must be devoted to the preparation and execution of the republican, district and communal plans.

Republican plans differ from local and, especially, communal plans both in importance and substance. Except for the fact that republican plans refer to only a segment of the country, and do not contain sections on such subjects as foreign trade, the balance of payments or general trends, they are not essentially different from the federal plan. As already indicated, they are prepared after, and take account of resources made available by, the federal plan. However, although the republics are required, through their own plan and by other means, to help carry out the objectives of the federal plan, they are under no legal obligation to harmonize their own plan with the federal plan. Since the federal plan provides for the distribution of most of the country's investment resources, the republican plan would hardly be realistic if its objectives deviated too greatly from those of the federal plan. Nevertheless, the republics remain free to set goals for themselves that go beyond the aims of the federal plan, if they have the additional resources to carry them out or are prepared to guarantee the achievement of higher goals with the funds made available to them through the federal plan. It is fair to say, however, that the republican plans, compared to the federal and communal plans, play a limited and residual role.

As the commune emerged as the basic unit of government, its plan took on greater importance, while the importance of the districts and their plans diminished correspondingly. Today the district plan may draw on district funds for transport, large schools, hospitals or cultural institutions, which provide services to the entire district. It may, however, also provide funds for services in communes which are not in a position to establish them and, in the case of backward communes, may also take the initiative in, and provide funds for, establishing new enterprises. The republican plan may be viewed as a territorial segment of the federal plan suitably modified in each case to take care of the special problems of each republic, while the district plan, in most cases, is merely the sum total of communal plans or is concerned with the general

interests of the communes associated in each district; in contrast
the communal plan has become the chief medium for realizing the
objectives of the federal plan.

While the district plan is usually general in nature, the communal plan is a detailed program of action for the economy in its
area. The communal plan concerns itself with the same economic
movements and deals with the same economic categories as the
federal and republican plans, but it includes many more specific
tasks, measures and regulations, set out in more detail, than in the
federal and republican plans. In particular, the communal plan
devotes greater attention than the plans of the republics and districts to those branches of the economy in which the commune has
been given wide responsibilities (such as commerce, catering,
handicrafts and local transport in the economic sector and public
utility services, schools, health, housing construction, cultural activities, and town planning in the social sector). The communal
plan provides both information and instructions which economic
organizations need to formulate their own investment and production plans; it allocates the commune's own funds between economic
and social purposes and it helps determine the distribution of
federal and other investment funds among existing enterprises and
the starting of new ones within its borders.

Since the fulfillment of the basic objectives in the federal plan
greatly depends on the plans of the communes, it is exceptionally
important to synchronize the communal plans, through the district
and republican plans, with the federal plan. Like the republican
plans, the communal (and the district) plans are not legally bound
by the federal plan, although the local governments, like the republics, are required by law to help carry out the federal plan's objectives. Here again, federal investment funds and measures to assure
their use for purposes laid out in the federal plan help keep local
plans in line with the federal plan; but once again, this does not
prevent the communes from setting objectives in their plans which
go beyond those in the federal plan, if they have resources to carry
them out or if they can give the necessary assurances to use federal
funds to achieve results above those set in the federal plan. Since
communal plans often go beyond the limits foreseen in the federal

plan, the totals of the estimates (e.g., of production, investment or growth) of all the communal plans or of all the districts or republican plans need not, and usually do not correspond to the totals in the federal plan. The order in which plans are adopted also contributes toward their interrelationship. The federal plan is the first to be adopted, then follow in order the republican, district and communal plans, and finally, come the plans of the economic organizations.

PLANS OF ECONOMIC ORGANIZATIONS

The plans which each economic organization prepares for its own operations are known as "independent" or "autonomous" plans because they are formulated by the economic organizations themselves independently of any governmental body. As we have seen, this does not mean that enterprises prepare their plans without regard to the social plans of the Federation, their republic, district or commune. Enterprises generally pay great attention to these plans, especially the plan of the commune in which they operate. Moreover, the appropriate economic association and chambers or trade unions, which assist enterprises in the preparation of their plans, do not fail to draw their attention, when necessary, to the objectives in the federal and other pertinent plans.

Of even greater importance in assuring general conformity between the objectives of the federal and the independent plans of the enterprises are the legal regulations, to be discussed in a later section, which all economic organizations must follow in distributing their income. Indeed, these regulations constitute the crucial means by which the independent plans are related to the federal plan. Nevertheless, if an enterprise chooses to go beyond the objectives of the social plans, no governmental body may object as long as the enterprise abides by the legal regulations. Since there are many instances where enterprises have done so, one must conclude that, within the framework of the legal rules, enterprises may plan and operate with a considerable measure of freedom.

The independent plans of enterprises are generally prepared in some detail and include programs for production, investment, employment and for distributing enterprise income. The plans of an enterprise remain provisional even after adoption. Economic organizations are not compelled, either by official plans or by other laws, to set any fixed production, employment or investment levels, nor are they required to submit any reports on the fulfillment of their plan. The enterprise is never under any legal obligation to carry out any plan it may have adopted since, as will be seen later, in the last analysis it is required to be guided in its activities by the demands of the market.

ANNUAL PLANS

For each year of the Five-Year Plan for 1947-51, a detailed annual operational plan was prepared to carry out the tasks of the Five-Year Plan and of the Key Investment Program which superseded it. The uncertainty surrounding the country's economic future after the breach in relations with the USSR, defense needs which fluctuated unpredictably with each flare-up of external political tensions and the necessity to adjust internally to the economic and political innovations of the period, made it difficult to plan ahead in the years from 1952 to 1956. In these years, therefore, only annual plans were published.

The annual federal plans for 1952 and 1953 were transitional plans which bridged the periods of administrative and decentralized planning. The 1952 plan was the first annual plan to be approved by the Federal People's Assembly. The 1952 and 1953 social plans reflected the new trend of the times toward decentralization, by permitting enterprises somewhat greater latitude to set prices in a more liberal market setting and allowing them more freedom to distribute earnings; but the plans also retained many administrative features characteristic of the period of centralized planning.

For although federal planners had broken with the system of detailed centralized planning, they were not yet ready to place great reliance on the market. They still set production quotas in the plans for each branch of the economy, although, in lieu of enterprise production targets fixed by central authorities, local authorities now set for each enterprise a required minimum percentage of utilization of its productive capacity. Since each enterprise was to be free to produce as much or as little as it wished, provided its total output reached the minimum level fixed by the planners, the new system allowed enterprises more freedom than before, especially in making decisions about the assortment of commodities they produced. Aside from the difficulty of measuring accurately the degree of utilization of capacity for each enterprise, the principle of minimum capacity utilization itself was too much in conflict with the spirit of the new system of self-management of enterprises to survive. In any event, the minima fixed seem not to have played an important part.

In order to obtain the distribution of the national income and the level of investment called for in the 1952 and 1953 plans, the planners also imposed on all public enterprises obligatory "rates of accumulation." These rates took the form of excise taxes, the proceeds of which were used to set aside funds for investment, depreciation and other selected purposes before any distribution of profits. The rates were related to the total wages paid out by enterprises and thus gave enterprises an incentive to dismiss unnecessary workers. In practice, however, rates of accumulation had to be varied greatly from one enterprise or group of enterprises to another, because of the difference in their technical efficiency, the rate at which they utilized their capacity, etc. The rates also had to be changed frequently to avoid inequities due to changing conditions. Consequently, it was still necessary for the authorities to intervene administratively in the affairs of enterprises to adjust the rates. Administrative methods also continued to be used to distribute the investment and other funds which enterprises were obliged to accumulate.

The Federal Social Plan for 1954 was the first to make a clean break with centralized administrative management of the economy and to face the implications of decentralization. Production goals for industry and agriculture and their branches were retained, but enterprises were no longer required to utilize specified minimum capacities; instead, they were left completely free to work out the ways in which they would expand their output. In lieu of the older administrative controls, the Plan introduced a series of financial measures or "economic instruments" for implementing its objectives by indirect means. These economic instruments required enterprises to make tax payments and other "contributions" which did not differ basically from what enterprises are normally required to make in most market economies. In brief, the new regulations provided that economic organizations would have to pay specified rates of interest on their capital assets; investment funds and working capital were to be advanced in the form of loans instead of grants; taxes were to be levied on enterprise sales and incomes, instead of on their wage bill, as before; a form of Ricardian rent was to be paid, the amount in each case to be determined by the extent to which an enterprise enjoyed more favorable natural conditions for realizing profits than other economic organizations in the same economic branch or group.

In the main, the annual plans enacted in 1955 and 1956 were similar in nature to the 1954 plan. Beginning in 1957, however, the annual plans became operational plans for implementing the Five-Year Plan for 1957-61 and, more recently, the Five-Year Plan for 1961-65. Annual plans now cover far fewer pages than formerly. For example, the Federal Social Plan for 1962 fills only 25 pages in the Official Gazette. The most recent annual federal plans have the following four parts:

1. A short qualitative statement of the basic aims and tasks of the plan for the ensuing year.

2. A statement of the proposed directions for the development of the economy in the ensuing year, including broad quantitative estimates of the expected expansion in gross product, national income, production, investments, personal consumption and the standard of living; federal expenditures for defense, administration and other non-investment purposes; and foreign trade, employment and productivity of labor.

3. The estimated growth of the volume and value of production by economic sectors.

4. An outline of the economic instruments adopted to implement the plan, such as the federal budget and the rules for the utilization of investment funds.

LONGER-TERM PLANS

By the end of 1956, the completion of the Key Investments Program, successful adaptation to economic and political reforms, improvement in the international outlook and greater experience in the technique of longer-term planning permitted the Federation to begin work on a five-year plan. Completed and approved by the Federal Assembly on December 4, 1957, and promulgated two days later, "The Social Plan of Economic Development of Yugoslavia from 1957 to 1961" bore little resemblance to the ill-fated Five-Year Plan for 1947-51, either in size, form or substance.

The Plan itself covered only about 40 small pages and was divided into four main parts. Part One contained a brief account of the problems which the economy faced, the potentialities for further growth and the plan's basic objectives. Part Two estimated the expected expansion of the gross social product and its components during the five-year period, the level of exports and imports and the balance of payments and the levels and compositions of investment, consumption and employment. Part Three described the expected expansion in output during the five years, by major economic sectors, while Part Four set forth objectives and means for extending the self-management of economic organizations, communes and other institutions and concluded with a brief statement calling on all social, political and economic organizations to prepare their own plans and to help realize the objectives of the federal plan. Appendix C outlines the major objectives of the Federal Social Plan for 1957-61. When it became evident that the objectives of the Five-Year Plan for 1957-61 would be achieved in four years, a draft of another five-year federal plan was published November 26, 1959, and adopted on December 28, 1960, for the period 1961-65. Appendix D outlines the major objectives of the Federal Social Plan for 1961-65.

As already indicated, beginning with the Federal Social Plan for 1957, the federal annual plans have become operational plans through which the objectives of the five-year plans are realized. However, except for a few key investments, even the annual plans do not list the projects by which the five-year plan objectives are

to be achieved. In the annual plans, means for implementing objectives may be included which do not figure in the Five-Year Plan,
or they may contain adjustments to compensate for shortfalls or
other unforeseen deviations from the aims of the longer-term plans.
As already indicated, the annual plans also contain a general statement of the economic instruments designed to insure realization of
the objectives in the annual plan, while the five-year plans do not.

The fact that new economic instruments are customarily announced with each annual plan has sometimes led enterprises to
contract operations toward the end of the year in anticipation of
further relaxation of restrictions. Yugoslav officials have discussed
ways of avoiding this. One way would be to introduce a "rolling
plan" which would consist of a revised five-year plan, embodying
the plan for the four remaining years of the existing Five-Year Plan
plus a plan for a fifth year. Under this system, which has other
merits as well, the instruments of economic policy could be issued
more easily as required without reference to the date when the
revised five-year plan was promulgated.

Even during the years 1952-56, when only annual plans were
adopted, the Federal Planning Institute prepared 10-year sector
programs to provide it with some perspective for further development in each economic sector and to furnish a better basis for
preparing the annual plans. A ten-year program for agricultural
development, which contemplated an increase of 50 percent in
agricultural production between 1953 and 1963, was even announced in October 1953, although the details of the program
were never made public and were used only in the Federal Planning Institute. In addition to the ten-year agricultural program,
tentative ten-year targets were also set in 1953 for the output of
electric power, coal, iron and steel, non-ferrous metals, engineering
industries, heavy chemicals and other sectors.

Experience gained with these longer-term plans established their
usefulness as planning tools. The Planning Institute has accordingly
prepared a long-term "perspective" plan[18] to run for a 20-year
period from 1960-80. It is not to be in as great detail as the

18. Yugoslav planners classify one-year plans as short-term, five-year plans as
medium-term, and 10- to 20-year plans as long term.

annual or even the five-year plans. Its main purpose is "to lend perspective," i.e., to project potential and desirable long-term directions of economic development. The plan could later be modified in the light of experience and then spelled out in progressively greater detail in the five-year and annual plans.

VI.

DECENTRALIZED PLANNING: IMPLEMENTATION OF PLANS

ONCE THE CENTRAL authorities had appreciably closed administrative channels through which they formerly imposed their will on enterprises, they had to find ways to bring about a widening and deepening of initiative in individuals, economic organizations and local governmental bodies. To accomplish this purpose, the authorities have developed a variety of means. These include: (1) active promotion of voluntary action, principally through the use of economic incentives and a broadening of the base of public participation in the planning process; (2) widening the scope of the market; (3) heavy reliance on economic and financial measures and mechanisms to balance supply and demand; and (4) utilization of economic, political and social organizations on various levels to arbitrate and reconcile differences between the social and independent plans.

STIMULATING VOLUNTARY ACTION BY THE USE OF ECONOMIC INCENTIVES

During the period of centralized planning, every citizen, civil servant and governmental unit was bound by law, "duty and honor" to discharge loyally the tasks imposed by the first Five-Year Plan and to comply with the decrees issued to enforce it. Everyone connected with the plan's operation was made individually responsible for the successful execution of the part of the Plan with which he was concerned, in what was, in essence, a "command economy."

50

Although there was little public discussion of the Plan while it was being formulated, as soon as it had been published every medium of communication was brought into play to keep the Plan and its objectives constantly before the public. Factories were encouraged to challenge each other in "socialist competition" to determine which could produce more. Outstanding workers were given the title of *udarnik* (shockworker), while those who helped rationalize production were awarded the title of *novator* (innovator) and their names were featured in the newspapers and over the radio.

In the period of decentralization, communication media are still used to appeal to workers and to the general public to bend every effort to make the plan a success. In great contrast with the past, however, is the present official realization that ". . . the maximum effort and initiative of the individual does not depend so much upon directives and control as it does upon the personal, economic, social, cultural and material interest of the worker who is working and creating in freedom."[19] This fresh point of view has made it possible to place the system of incentives on a firmer foundation than exhortation and zeal.

During the period of centralized planning, some attempt had been made to relate individual earnings to productivity, but the prevailing feeling that everyone should be paid according to need rather than ability tended to level wages and salaries. Differences in earnings based on the character of work performed were often greatly reduced by family allowances. Each worker received a flat wage rate which depended on the class of work he did and what amounted to an equal share in the profits of his enterprise, regardless of his individual contribution. As late as 1952, salaries of managers of enterprises in small firms were fixed at a level no more than three times the wages of unskilled workers and no more than five times in the largest firms. This set an upper limit equivalent to US$65 to US$110 per month on salaries. "The consequences were lack of responsibility, lack of initiative, lack of incentives, and,

19. McVicker, Charles P. *Titoism; Pattern for International Communism.* New York, St. Martin's Press, 1957, p. 61, quoting Vice-President Kardelj.

only after all this had become obvious,"[20] did this lead in 1957 to greater differentiation in wages and salaries. Socialism was re-defined as " 'a social system based on socialized means of produc-tion and in which production is directed by the producers them-selves in association, and distribution takes place on the principle... 'to each according to his work' ...'."[21] Although family allotments still have some counterbalancing effect, the growing spread be-tween the earnings of the unskilled and the highly skilled, especially if premiums based on output per man are included, support Yugo-slav claims that the system of wage payments now in effect adheres to the principle that the individual worker is rewarded according to the amount and kind of work performed.

However, the distribution of earnings on the basis of individual, rather than group, productivity and output has also had some un-desirable repercussions, since it has tended to make workers con-centrate on their own jobs and neglect the teamwork needed to raise group productivity. To correct this defect and to create a situation in which "the direct producer also becomes a manager, a fact which, in our conditions, is regarded as a decisive factor for further development,"[22] a new system ("distribution according to complex output") has been introduced. Under it, the income of each worker is tied, not only to the income of the enterprise and his own productivity, but also to the efficiency of the department or division of the enterprise in which he works. In discussing the new system of distributing personal incomes, the Yugoslavs admit that "in developing the criteria of work for individuals and individ-ual productive departments (we call them economic units) we have made use of the experience of both socialist and capitalist coun-tries."[23] The system, which involves the division of an enterprise into units, each of which is governed by its workers, has been on

20. Horvat and Rascovic. "Workers' Management in Yugoslavia: a Comment," pp. 197-198.

21. Deleon, Aser. "Workers' Management," in "Collective Economy in Yugo-slavia," p. 148, quoting the Programme of the League of Communists of Yugo-slavia.

22. Spiljak, Mika. "Remuneration or Distribution According to Work," *Review of International Affairs* (Beograd), Vol. 12, No. 259, January 20, 1961, p. 14.

23. *Ibid.*

trial operation in many enterprises for about two years and is now being extended to others. Even the railroads and airlines have been divided into several divisions. This development has caused some Yugoslavs to become concerned that the trend toward decentralization may, at least in cases where unitary operation is economically desirable, lead to disadvantages which outweigh the benefits to be obtained from improved divisional cooperation.

The use of pecuniary incentives, especially the principle of making earnings depend on work performed, has also been applied to government and social welfare institutions. Employees of the federal civil service, who have until recently been paid according to a standard wage schedule, are hereafter to receive remuneration on the basis of a two-part schedule. One part will consist of a guaranteed basic salary, varying according to the job, the qualifications and experience of the incumbent; the second part will be a variable amount paid monthly and based on the efficiency and initiative of the jobholder as determined by fixed criteria. Even doctors in publicly owned hospitals are to be given an opportunity to earn bonuses above their basic wages on the basis of increased work performed.

It is, however, in their application to enterprise earnings as the guiding principle of production policy that economic incentives have been developed most extensively. Two kinds of incentives have been devised to stimulate enterprises to greater production and more rational use of their productive capacities and labor. The purpose of one set of measures is to promote increased output by levying fixed charges on an enterprise, irrespective of its volume of output. These include a depreciation charge on its capital equipment, interest on borrowed funds, a tax on its fixed and working capital and (until 1961) a land tax. Since the proportional burden of these charges declines as output rises, it is in the interest of an enterprise to make the greatest use of its capacity in order to increase income and, thereby, the potential income per person employed. The second set of measures has been incorporated in the tax system to promote the allocation of enterprise income to investment purposes. Thus, a personal income tax must be paid on enterprise earnings distributed to workers, but (until 1961) none had been levied on earnings set aside for investment. Workers and management with the long view have thereby been encouraged to postpone some increase in current personal earnings in order to increase their future earning potential by increasing investments.

STIMULATING VOLUNTARY ACTION BY WIDENING PARTICIPATION IN THE PLANNING PROCESS

In addition to the use of pecuniary incentives, the authorities seek to stimulate popular interest in the federal and other governmental plans by increasing the numbers who participate in self-management of economic organizations and local government. Each workers' council must discuss and approve the plan of its economic organization and each representative body must discuss and approve the plan of its own local government or republic. The avowed official objective is to get every worker to participate in self-management of enterprises at some time. Since one-third of the members of each workers' council is elected each year and no member may be re-elected more than once immediately after serving his first term, most if not all of the workers may eventually participate. The extensive system of representative bodies in the federal republican, district and communal governments also involves an increasing number of people in the planning activities of these groups.

Of course, the election of large numbers to serve on various bodies does not by itself ensure meaningful participation of those elected. Yugoslav authorities recognize, especially, that effective:

> development of the workers' councils, must also be considered as a gradual process and one of long duration. For the dangers are numerous: formalism in management, reduction of democracy to a mere formula, failure to see existing rights and make full use of them. There are working collectivities whose organs of management have become bureaucratized, i.e., isolated from their collectives; there are managers and experts who, either intentionally or because they are incapable, prevent the members of the workers' councils and working collectivities from having access to an understanding of the essential data on the economic development of the

undertaking; there are collectives as yet unexperienced where the managers have sovereign power of decision and impose their will on the organs of management; there are cases where the workers lack the required knowledge and have not yet been able to acquire sufficient experience to manage the undertaking's affairs successfully; there are undertakings where the workers' councils cannot obtain the informative material which would enable them to follow the life of the undertaking and the evolution of production and distribution, which naturally hinders effective decision; there are workers who do not dare to take an active part in important decisions, etc. . . . But these are only inevitable phenomena which bear witness to the difficulty, the complexity and the slowness of the struggle for democracy, that is to say, for the development of a political mechanism truly based on the activity of thousands and thousands of individuals.[24]

THE MARKET

Two guiding principles of the period of centralized management and planning were the superfluity of the market in a socialist economy and the rejection of the price system. The central authority relied on a tight quota system to channel producer goods and scarce raw materials to enterprises at prices calculated by the planners and on a comprehensive rationing system to distribute limited quantities of consumer goods at fixed prices. Those who obtained their livelihood in the private sector had to rely on high priced goods which found their way into a free market, where price fluctuations were carefully insulated from the rest of the economy. In practice, however, even workers in the socialized sector often were compelled to supplement their meager rations in the free market.

The changeover from strict *dirigisme* to the current "planned market economy" went hand in hand with the evolution of the system of self-management. As the price system was permitted to re-establish itself, it became possible gradually to relinquish direct controls and to replace them with indirect economic measures. The

24. Deleon, Aser. "Workers' Management," in "Collective Economy in Yugoslavia," pp. 153-154.

usefulness of self-correcting market forces in optimizing allocation
of resources was increasingly acknowledged and the virtues of
competition were officially extolled. The authorities have not only
permitted enterprises to compete with each other; they have encouraged it as a means of increasing output and reducing costs. Some
Yugoslav planners contend that planning performs a corrective
function by shifting resources to compensate for socially undesirable results of market automaticity. However, the most common
view among planners at present is that the market now "plays an
important role in correcting the planned proportions of distribution
and consumption, since it is precisely on the market that a direct
check can be made as to whether these proportions have in fact
been established in accordance with the action of economic laws
and whether the measures necessary to enforce them have been
taken."[25]

The market for capital goods is still largely determined by the
allocation of investment funds and productive capacity. With only
minor exceptions, however, market demand for consumption goods
is now considered to be the main determinant of the volume, quality
and structure of output of economic enterprises. Since the federal
plans estimate what the demand is likely to be in each sector, in
some sectors in greater detail than in others, they furnish producers
with clues of the likely demand for products they manufacture.[26]
In addition, a large number of fairs and industrial shows, as well
as contractual agreements with buyers, give enterprises a workable
knowledge of the volume and quality of output they may expect to
sell in relation to their competitors.

Because of "human fallibility" and the "impossibility of foresee-
ing all eventualities," each federal plan sets aside specific quantities
of various commodities (e.g., coal, wheat and petroleum), and
money as "social reserves" and "unallocated resources" to take care
of contingencies. Part of these reserves is kept as a safeguard
against unforeseeable events (e.g., floods and droughts or a

25. Sirotkovic, Yakov. "Planned Economy in Yugoslavia," in "Collective
Economy in Yugoslavia," p. 140.
26. The levels of consumption fixed in the plans are based on the level of output. By imposing taxes and by other means purchasing power is equated with the
planned output of goods and services.

deterioration in the balance of payments), and part is distributed during the implementation of the plan for various types of consumption. A portion of the reserves is also available if authorities feel it is necessary to intervene in the market during the execution of the plan. Yugoslav planners see the market reserves as a cushion against "the effect of the noneconomic factors and eventual unforeseen difficulties in the implementation of the plan" which makes it possible to implement the plan "without superfluous intervention on the part of the central organs."[27]

With the coming of competition in the market, trade names and licensing of manufactures by patent holders reappeared. Competition among enterprises has led to a rise in the number of enterprises in each branch of the economy and to a steady improvement in the supply, variety and quality of goods rather than to a decline in prices. The number of enterprises has increased through the division of large, monopolistic firms into smaller units, as well as through the creation of new concerns. Reduced costs of production have not been reflected in lower prices because inflation induced by high investments and high taxes wiped out reductions in costs of production. But the effects of competition, as a means for getting more abundant supply and diversification of products, is in such happy contrast with the mediocrity and standardization of monopolistic enterprises during the period of centralized planning that consumers (whose real income has been rising steadily) generally feel that the products they buy are worth the prices they pay.[28]

27. Sergej Krajer (at the time), Director of the Federal Planning Office, in "Review of International Affairs," (Beograd), May 1, 1958, p. 17.

28. One Yugoslav economist, reminiscing about the past and contrasting it with the present, writes: "One can scarcely look with nostalgia upon the times when the entire city of Zagreb (350,000 inhabitants) was supplied by a single large retail business enterprise and one consumers' cooperative, and when in 1947, the two largest beaches on the Adriatic Coast were entitled to no more than one type of cake a day in all restaurants, cafes and bakeries, all made in the same place. The monopoly of an industry by one firm for one product was achieved as in a treatise of political economy, but the cakes were not very appetizing. Today the savings of large-scale production are less, but the cakes are better." Bicanic, Rudolf. "La Concurrence Socialiste en Yougoslavie," Economie Appliquée, Archives de l'Institut de Science Economique Appliquée (Paris), Vol. 9, No. 3, July/September 1956, p. 343 (translation).

If market prices govern the distribution of resources, efficient planning and allocation of resources depend on the freedom of the price system from distortions. Considerable progress has been made in Yugoslavia toward creating a free market economy which permits prices to be adjusted freely in accordance with consumers' preferences. Physical rationing has been eliminated and consumers are free to buy any goods they can find in the market. Enterprises compete for factors of production by paying more to attract sellers, technicians or workers, who are in turn free to seek out the firm which pays the most.

A substantial number of domestic prices are, nevertheless, still subject to direct controls and, until 1961, international transactions were carried out under a complex system of multiple exchange rates and trade restrictions. Except in the case of public utilities and other public monopolies, these direct interferences with market forces are considered to be temporary expedients required to counteract inflationary tendencies and the high propensity to import which accompany the accelerated growth of the economy. The multiple exchange system in effect until 1961 employed a large series of "coefficients" which were essentially a series of import taxes or export subsidies. By raising prices of some imports, they discouraged the inflow of nonessentials and commodities manufactured in Yugoslavia and by providing subsidies on certain exports, they permitted Yugoslav enterprises to sell their high-cost output at competitive world price levels. The general domestic effect of the multiple exchange rate system was to lower domestic prices of agricultural commodities, especially essential foods, fuel, raw materials, some semi-fabricated products and needed capital goods below world prices and to raise domestic prices of luxury imports (e.g., automobiles), fabricated consumer goods, exportable capital goods and luxury goods to levels sometimes greatly above world prices. The difference between domestic and world prices for some of these commodities was over 200 percent and since foreign trade accounts for about 18 percent of Yugoslavia's social product, trade restrictions and multiple rates had an important effect on the level of supply and prices in the domestic market.

Ceiling prices, often accompanied by turnover taxes, have been imposed by the Federation on domestically produced or imported commodities in short supply (e.g., wheat, corn, tobacco and its products, sugar, industrial salt, kerosene, coal, pig iron, semi-fabricated iron products, steel, aluminum, lead and some chemicals), which cover an estimated 26 to 28 percent of the domestic production of raw materials and semi-manufactures. Price controls are also imposed to keep the cost of living in line with wages (house rent, electricity, public transportation), to control the profits of national monopolies (copper), or to stimulate exports of certain goods (e.g., capital goods). For an extended list of other commodities (including window glass, cutlery, bicycles, refrigerators, paints, rayon, silk and shoes), accounting for less than half of total consumption, enterprises must temporarily give one month's notice and justification to governmental authorities before increasing prices. While the authorities seldom refuse to grant price increases when requested, the requirement of proof that a price increase is necessary undoubtedly tends to stabilize prices. In order to stimulate agricultural production, the Federation also maintains support prices for certain agricultural products, including cereals, wine, beans and high-quality livestock and provides certain subsidies (e.g., for synthetic fertilizer).

Price and exchange controls have seriously distorted some prices and furnished misleading incentives to consumption, current production and, most importantly, to investment; nevertheless, it remains true that for most commodities, prices are determined freely by supply and demand. Moreover, the number of commodities affected and the extent to which they have been controlled have been declining since the beginning of 1958. At the beginning of 1960, controlled rents were increased by 150 percent, home power rates by about 130 percent and railway freight rates by 15 percent. While further increases are necessary before these services furnish a return which is comparable to those in other sectors, the increases at least raised prices to a level which equals current costs and depreciation and permits some return on invested capital.

The Federation's announced objective is to continue to reduce administrative intervention in the market. In November 1959,

Yugoslavia became an associate member of the General Agreement on Tariffs and Trade under conditions which require her to abolish most direct controls on imports and foreign trade. At the end of 1960, the Government, after consulting the International Monetary Fund, also adopted a far-reaching foreign exchange and import reform program to be put into effect over the next few years. The reform provided for the introduction of a uniform rate of exchange of 750 dinars to the dollar; replacement of the system of coefficients with a customs tariff system for imports; replacement of coefficients by a uniform clearing rate with premiums for some exports; removal of some restrictions on imports and a simpler system of allocating foreign exchange. These measures, if carried out, should gradually bring Yugoslav prices into line with world prices. Yugoslav authorities have also indicated that they intend in the future to influence domestic prices largely through indirect financial, credit, trade and fiscal measures. Nevertheless, serious problems remain. Since Yugoslav exports are not yet competitive in Western markets, it will not be easy to eliminate the heavily unfavorable balance of trade. In seeking to solve the balance of payments problem, authorities are considering a variety of solutions, including " 'offers of certain foreign [private] investors for the construction of tourist facilities in Yugoslavia.' "[29] Meanwhile, the authorities consider it necessary to retain import quotas and bilateral trade agreements.

Under the system of decentralized decision-making, interest rates were reintroduced as a cost of capital. However, they do not yet play a decisive role in the allocation of investment and are not an important factor in production costs, since the federal plans allocate investment funds to the various sectors; moreover, investment funds are loaned at subsidized rates (e.g., 2 percent for electrification, 3 percent for agriculture, construction, transport and commerce, and 4 percent for industry and mining). Some attempt has been made to set interest rates competitively within the allocations made by the federal plans through a system by which loans are made to borrowers who, among other things, are willing to pay the highest interest rate; but most interest rates are still fixed at subsidized levels.

29. From an article by Tanyug, the official press agency, as reported by *The New York Times,* March 11, 1962.

Market forces are also weak in the case of land and other natural resources. Although agricultural land may be bought and sold freely, private holdings are generally restricted to the 10 hectares already mentioned. Full economic rent is generally not charged for land used by commerce and industry, and in spite of attempts to levy Ricardian rent on enterprises enjoying inherent advantages, workers in mines with richer ores generally are paid more than workers in mines with poorer ores, even though the former are no more efficient.

Although the Federation has set minimum wage rates as guarantees for workers, they are so far below the levels paid by most enterprises that they have had little effect in determining the earnings of most workers. Each enterprise, in cooperation with its economic chamber, sets rates which take into account the kind of work performed, efficiency (i.e., the extent to which output exceeds established norms) and the going rates in the industry. However, since (as will be seen later) wages and salaries are not chargeable to the cost of production, but to the income of the enterprise after it makes payments for materials, depreciation, taxes and certain other charges, the amounts earned by workers and employees ultimately depend on the income of their enterprise.

THE INSTRUMENTS OF ECONOMIC POLICY

In the period of administrative planning, economic organizations, political entities and others charged with carrying out portions of the Five-Year Plan were held fully accountable for achieving the targets which the planners had more or less arbitrarily imposed upon them. The planning authorities themselves, although executors of the Plan, admitted to no responsibility for failures. In sharp contrast, the planning authorities now prepare the plans without fixed targets of any kind for producing units. Instead, they help devise economic instruments by which individuals and economic organizations are indirectly induced to take actions which will lead, through the operation of the market, to fulfillment of the plans.

As we have seen, the state generally does not dictate to an economic organization what, or at what price, it is to produce, buy or sell; it seeks, instead, to influence production by regulating the distribution of enterprise incomes through the use of a series of economic instruments. A key role in this process is assigned to the tax system, which serves as a tool of economic and social policy to regulate purchasing power, control monopoly and influence the formation of market prices as well as to produce funds for investment and government budgets. In addition to taxes, the economic instruments include compulsory deductions from incomes of economic organizations, regulations which govern the distribution of their income remaining after taxes and compulsory deductions, as well as credit and monetary measures.

The instruments of economic policy used in Yugoslavia resemble those of any modern market economy; they are unique because they are designed primarily to bring about a distribution of enterprise incomes to achieve the targets, particularly those for investment, in the federal plans. The instruments must be skillfully designed to stimulate the initiative of economic organizations and workers without endangering the basic aims of the plans. This requires a nice balance between the conflicting and common interests of the enterprise and the community.

The problem is complicated by the fact that the economic instruments must, to avoid administrative intervention, be framed in terms of "proportions" or percentages applicable to unknown quantities, which materialize later from the operations of many economic organizations. This fact, as well as changes in targets and conditions, requires that economic instruments remain under constant review. They are generally revised every year and they may even be modified, if necessary, in the course of implementing an annual plan.

CHARGES ON ENTERPRISES

Regulations in effect before 1961 generally required each enterprise in the socialized sector to defray out of its total receipts a depreciation allowance on fixed assets; the cost of materials and services used in production; interest on investment and short-term loans; a turnover tax in certain cases; a tax on fixed and working capital (in addition to the depreciation and interest charges mentioned above); a land tax and miscellaneous taxes and membership fees. Mines and petroleum companies which realized abnormally high profits because of favorable conditions of operation also paid a form of Ricardian rent. A progressive income tax was then generally applied on the basis of the relationship of the balance ("income of the enterprise" in Yugoslav terminology) to the minimum wages paid by the enterprise. From what remained (called "net income"), the enterprise next had to pay minimum wages (or the higher norms it may have fixed), after which the worker's council could allocate the remainder, either to supplemental wages and salaries or to the enterprise's reserve, fixed assets, working assets or social welfare funds.

In order to provide stronger incentives to enterprises to reduce costs by economizing on manpower, investing in productive equipment and otherwise increasing productivity, a series of significant changes was made early in 1961 in the regulations governing the incomes of enterprise. The most important change involved the replacement of the progressive income tax by a flat tax on gross incomes, supplemented by an excess profits tax to catch windfall profits when income exceeded 6 percent of invested capital. Amortization allowances for equipment in the transport and metallurgical industries and in agriculture were increased to allow quicker replacement of capital equipment in these branches of the economy. The distinction made in former tax regulations between funds used for fixed investment and those used for working capital, which had led enterprises to overinvest in fixed capital in relation to working capital, was abolished. In order to induce enterprises to make more effective use of invested capital, the 3 percent tax on such capital was increased to about 4 percent. The separate tax on land was eliminated and the value of the land owned by the enterprise is now included in the tax base for the 4 percent tax. Other new regulations, which have the effect of greatly increasing the cost of borrowed capital funds, are intended to stimulate investors to accumulate and use more of their own capital than in the past and to repay loans from the various investment funds more quickly. Since republics, districts and communes received most of their revenues prior to 1961 from the amount of wages paid out by enterprises, local governments tended to put pressure on enterprises to employ additional workers. The new regulations, intended to get local governments to encourage the accumulation of capital by enterprises, provide that republics and communes, in addition to receiving 13 percent of the wage bill of enterprises, also are entitled to the proceeds of a 20 percent tax on the amounts allocated by enterprises to their investment funds. Appendix E outlines in greater detail the 1961 and former regulations affecting the distribution of enterprise incomes.

While the actual distribution of an enterprise's net income is, in principle, left to the judgment of its workers' council, specific rules also govern this final distribution in order to assure that certain minima are set aside from income for investment and other purposes. An enterprise whose net income is at least 40 percent higher than its net wage and salary payments must put a part of its net income into its reserve fund until the fund has been built up to varying proportions (10 to 40 percent) of its working capital in the last three years. Special legal provisions also give general directions which the workers' council is expected to follow when allocating the net income of the enterprise. Thus, that part of the net income which has been earned as a result of the special effort of the enterprise and its workers, either through an increase in productivity or otherwise, may be distributed as wages and salaries or allocated to its social welfare fund, while that part which arises from improved business or market conditions must be allocated to the investment or reserve fund of the enterprise. Obviously, there is room for difference of opinion in dividing the net income of an enterprise according to the rule, but should the workers' council lean too far in one direction or another, the communal producers' council, the local trade union and the economic associations to which the enterprise belongs, are likely to exercise countervailing pressures.

It is therefore apparent that there are a series of checks on the principle of enterprise autonomy, at least as regards the way it may distribute its net income. These restrictions are defended on the ground that it is necessary to educate the workers to look at their enterprise not only as wage earners but also as sharers in its profits. It is largely for this reason that wages are treated as a part of the residual income of enterprises and not as a cost of production. The authorities believe that workers must learn to sacrifice immediate gain for higher and more consistent earnings in the future, as they must also learn to accept the fact that the manager, technicians and skilled staff must be paid salaries higher than their own wages, if adequate management is to be obtained.

These things are being learned but not as fast in some enterprises as in others. In 1954, free and easy distribution of enterprise profits by workers' councils made it necessary to enact laws which provided for prior deductions from enterprise incomes before the workers' council could distribute additional earnings to workers and employees. At first, also, the proportion of enterprise earnings which the authorities permitted workers' councils to distribute was small. It was gradually increased until, in 1960, it averaged about 20 percent of the total income of enterprises. Beginning in 1961, the proportion left at the disposal of the workers' council was almost trebled to average 55 percent of total enterprise earnings. Further increases in this proportion are expected when the new Yugoslav constitution goes into effect in 1962 and planners promise that "in the future one may expect all funds to be administered by the working collective."[30]

Although the fixed charges on enterprise income are numerous and add up to substantial amounts, they are conceived and have been adjusted over the years so as not to be unduly burdensome on an enterprise which is operating with reasonable efficiency. The rules for distributing enterprise income have been formulated so as to leave the enterprise a larger share of net income, if its labor productivity is rising and the operations of the enterprise are profitable. For small handicraft, commercial, catering and other enterprises, contributions from enterprise income for interest on fixed and working capital, turnover and other taxes are levied in a lump sum,

30. Horvat and Rascovic. "Workers' Management in Yugoslavia: a Comment," p. 198.

as agreed upon between the enterprise and the local commune. This not only provides the flexibility needed to meet the variable conditions of small and local businesses, but furnishes them with an inducement to increase earnings above the level on which their lump payment has been based. For larger and more profitable enterprises, the law provides that, if they realize a more favorable ratio of income to total wages and salaries than the average for the previous two years, they may retain a part of the excess to distribute as part of their net income.

Moreover, because it is official policy to allow enterprises as much autonomy as possible in order to stimulate individual and enterprise initiative, workers' councils have been allowed to vote themselves substantial proportions of enterprise income in the form of supplemental wages and salaries. In 1959, for example, an average of 32.5 percent of enterprise incomes (after deducting depreciation and the cost of raw material used) constituted take-home pay for workers and employees, in addition to the 15 percent of enterprise income which had to be paid for social security and personal income taxes withheld at the source.

CREDIT AND BANKING SYSTEM

Under the previous system, the Yugoslav banking system was essentially a means of controlling production and investment; under the prevailing system the banks, especially the National Bank of Yugoslavia and the Yugoslav Investment Bank, continue to play important roles in influencing production and investment. In addition to exercising the normal functions of a central bank, including those of a bank of issue, the National Bank has great powers of economic and financial control. In cooperation with the interested federal agencies, it influences production by allocating foreign exchange, which economic organizations must sell to it. Between 1952 and 1954, the National Bank was practically the sole dispenser of investment and short-term credit for working capital. This arrangement proved inadequate and, beginning in 1954, a series of separate specialized banks were established to extend loans for investment, foreign trade, agriculture and other purposes. Under new regulations these banks will generally grant loans to communal banks, but may also make loans directly to enterprises in certain cases. Nevertheless, with the exception of the Investment Bank, which operates as an independent entity, the National Bank still dominates the banking system. Through the credits it extends, credit ceilings and reserve requirements which it may impose on other banks and other powers which it possesses, the National Bank is in position to determine that the volume and general direction of the country's short-term bank credit operation conform to the objectives of the federal plans.

Besides the indirect check which the unified credit system gives the National Bank over economic organizations, the Bank exercises powerful direct controls over them through a system of "social control of accounts." At the end of each day, every economic organization is normally required to deposit its income in the National Bank or one of its branches. Most domestic and foreign payments by economic organizations must be made through the Bank, to which full information must be furnished on the purpose of each payment. In addition, each economic organization must file with the Bank a monthly report showing its cash inflows and outflows in detail and quarterly balance sheets. The Bank is authorized to audit the accounts of any economic organization.

The money deposited is divided into separate accounts, each designated for a specific purpose, e.g., depreciation fund, business fund, costs of operations account, etc. The National Bank seeks to ensure that each account is used only for the prescribed purpose. As a consequence of its social accounting controls, the National Bank not only has a daily record of the flow of funds in the social and governmental sectors of the economy, which constitutes a valuable planning tool,[31] but also the means by which the federal

31. For example, in 1961, the National Bank completed a seven-volume summary of the most important items in the 1960 balance sheets of some 7,000 enterprises whose output accounted for over 90 percent of the country's social product in 1960. The summary, which shows major balance sheet figures by enterprise, branch and sector of the economy, commune, district, republic and nation, should prove to be valuable for planning purposes by permitting regional and other comparisons of capital-labor and other ratios, etc.

planning authorities can, if necessary, restrict the use of certain funds. As a matter of fact, almost every annual plan in recent years has called for the blocking or freezing of some funds of economic organizations to reduce potential investment or excessive demand. Local governments are also required to set up a portion of their incomes as reserves. By blocking these reserves, most of which would be used for investment, central authorities may, if necessary, further reduce investment. Since there are over 23,000 economic organizations whose accounts must be monitored, it is clear that the job is not easy. In practice, the National Bank has not been able to exercise the control over the financial activities of enterprises which its powers make possible. As a result, economic organizations probably have more freedom of decision than the regulations would indicate. Steps are being taken to improve the Bank's organization and a separate department has recently been set up to take charge of social control of enterprise accounts.

The new and more conventional part which money is coming to play in the economy is also making necessary changes in the character of the National Bank and its staff. Before 1952 and to a somewhat lesser extent until 1960, money was employed largely as an accounting device and as a means for limiting effective demand to available supplies of goods. However, beginning in 1960 and especially in 1961, a series of official measures resulted in greatly broadening the role of money in the Yugoslav economy. The number of accounts which each enterprise had to maintain in the National Bank was substantially reduced by consolidation and enterprises were allowed greater discretion in disbursing deposits (e.g., funds deposited in *giro* (demand deposit) accounts, which formerly could only be used for current expenses, may now also be disbursed for investment and consumption). The recent substitution of a unitary exchange rate for the former system of multiple coefficients has also greatly enhanced the significance of money in foreign trade.

Since the importance of money in the economy is expected to grow, new economic instruments, which are both more complex and more flexible than those formerly employed, must be devised. To enable the National Bank better to regulate the volume of credit

under the new conditions, the Bank is being reorganized to conform more closely to the usual model of a central bank. While it
will continue to supervise the accounts of enterprises, it will no
longer grant credits for working capital directly to enterprises.
Attempts are being made to add substantially to the small staff of
trained statisticians and economists now in the Bank in order to
improve and enlarge the collection and analysis of financial statistics, relate them more closely to the national accounts and utilize
these data to formulate economic instruments more suitable to a
money economy.

INVESTMENT: FINANCING INVESTMENT

In the process of decentralization, the way in which capital funds
were mobilized and distributed underwent radical changes. Before
decentralization, investment funds were accumulated in the federal
budget from enterprise profits, taxes, social insurance funds and
loans, and distributed by the central authorities for investment, more
or less under their direct supervision. Under the new system, most
investment funds are accumulated and invested by enterprises and
communes.

The nature of governmental budgets also underwent basic
changes. Budgets of the republics and local governments are no
longer mere segments of the federal budget. Each governmental
unit now has its own independent budget, subject to the control of
its own legislative body. The federal budget, now much smaller
and less important than it was prior to 1953, when it was practically
the sole source of all public investment expenditures, is now mainly
concerned with government administration, defense, the construction of schools, hospitals and other health institutions, and government buildings. Federal budgetary receipts come from the turnover tax, a portion of the tax on incomes of enterprises and, to a
much less extent, from such sources as profits from foreign exchange
operations, custom receipts and other miscellaneous items.

The budgets of republics, districts and communes share varying
proportions of the turnover tax, the tax on enterprise incomes and

proceeds of the income tax on peasants, craftsmen and the professions in the private sector. In addition, the commune obtains budgetary revenues from a local turnover tax, death duties, inheritance and gift taxes, and public fees. The federal budget provides some subsidies for the republics, which are also allocated to district and communal budgets. Local government budgets finance basic services and cultural activities, public elementary education, health and welfare.

Government budgets now account for only a small percentage of capital formation. "Noneconomic" investments (for health, education, social welfare and administration) are still made from budgetary resources of the federal, republic and local governments, usually without obligation to repay. On the other hand, investments in the economy are almost always made in the form of repayable long-term loans from non budgetary federal, republic or local "social investment funds." These funds have been separated from budgets in order to make it easier for them to be administered by banks, which have been found to be better able than governments to check on the propriety of projects and the responsibility of their sponsors from an economic, rather than a political, point of view. There are also housing funds and "special social funds" at different governmental levels, with resources earmarked to finance investments in specific fields like agricultural development, road construction and maintenance, water supply, research, communal fire departments, fisheries and wildlife, etc. Financing from these sources usually does not involve reimbursement by beneficiaries. In addition to investments made from governmental investment funds, economic organizations also invest in the economy. In 1959, "noneconomic" investments financed from all governmental budgetary resources accounted for only 9 percent of total investment. Investment in the economy from federal, republican and local social investment funds came to 47 percent and from resources of enterprises to 27 percent of total investment. The remaining investment came from housing funds (9 percent) autonomous institutes and special social funds (each of which provided 4 percent of total investment).

Federal investment resources are concentrated in a General

Investment Fund, which is largely fed by the proceeds of the tax on the fixed and working assets of enterprises, a portion of the proceeds from the federal tax on enterprise incomes (after 1961, from the flat 15 percent tax on such incomes), the tax on excess profits, a portion of the differential tax on mining and petroleum income, counterpart funds of foreign loans, reparations and restitution payments and other contributions from abroad and repayments on loans previously made from the General Investment Fund.

Social investment funds of republics and communes generally share the proceeds of the tax (levied for the first time in 1961) on the part of net income which enterprises allocate to their investment and social welfare funds. Investment funds of republics and communes also get a portion of the receipts from the differential tax on mining and petroleum profits and they also share the proceeds from the 15 percent tax on personal incomes of workers.

Communal and district social investment and special funds are held and managed by communal banks, under the direction of the local peoples' committees. In addition to acting as the fiscal and accounting agents for the districts and communes, the communal banks accept deposits from the public and provide investment and working capital credit to the retailing, hotel and handicraft trades, and consumption credits to consumers. With greater decentralization in investment activities, the importance of the communal banks as a source of investment financing for all enterprises is increasing.

Each annual federal plan estimates the resources of the federal General Investment Fund, indicates the sources from which the Fund will obtain its resources and allocates them by economic sectors and sometimes by sub-sectors and, in the case of less developed regions, by geographic areas. The Investment Bank is responsible for making loans from the General Investment Fund according to these allocations. In addition to administering the General Investment Fund, the Bank has administered the investment and housing funds of the six republics and the two autonomous regions, in accordance with their respective plans. The Bank extends loans mostly to industry for the acquisition or improvement of fixed assets and to provide working capital. The Bank also allocates the foreign exchange needed for investment.

Although normally bound by the allocations in the plans, the Investment Bank, because of its experience, has played an important role in setting the allocations. It is also expected and permitted to exercise judgment in making loans. If, in its opinion, a federal plan does not take adequate account of investment requirements in a specific sector or sectors, it may, after consulting the Federal Planning Institute and other federal agencies concerned, deviate from the plan. Until about the end of 1956, federal investment funds were mainly allocated to projects which had been centrally planned. Even since 1956, the Federation has continued, in the main, to take responsibility for and finance projects in the less developed areas and for highways, railways and electric power systems which extend beyond the territory of one republic. However, for most new projects, federal policy requires that investment decisions be decentralized as much as possible.

The authorities correctly assumed that economic organizations would need no special stimulus to invest their own funds to modernize or expand their own plant capacity, since both modernization and expansion held promise of greater profits for enterprises and higher earnings for workers. On the other hand, existing enterprises generally had little reason to establish new enterprises or even branches of their own firms, since the laws governing enterprises provide that once established, new enterprises or branches of existing enterprises are to be governed by their own workers' councils and management boards. Nor was it likely that new enterprises in sufficient number would be started by groups of qualified citizens at their own initiative, even though there is no legal bar to their doing so, since they would also have to turn over management of the new enterprise to its workers as soon as the enterprise was in operation.

Since the founder of a new undertaking must also guarantee the funds required to equip the new enterprise (which come mainly in the form of long-term loans from the various investment funds and occasionally by way of a gift from a public authority), there was no practical alternative to having most new enterprises founded by a public authority. In line with federal policy on decentralization, the communes have been given the main task of initiating new enterprises. They are the logical authorities to start enterprises since their tax receipts increase with individual and enterprise earnings in their territories. For the few projects which are beyond the capabilities of a commune, districts, and especially republics, take the initiative.

Although problems involving decentralized initiation of large-scale projects have not yet been completely resolved, the system by which communes and republics are stimulated to initiate new projects must be judged one of the most successful and dynamic aspects of the Yugoslav economy. Communes and republics often originate projects themselves. An important role is also played by consulting firms which have sprung up to aid governmental bodies start new enterprises. These consulting firms frequently initiate and prepare plans for new projects which they then seek to get communes or others to sponsor. They investigate market possibilities, compile financial and other data needed to obtain capital and bank loans and provide the technical aid needed to get an enterprise started. There is no dearth of investment projects prepared for the sectors which the federal plans schedule for expansion. On the contrary, it has become necessary on occasion to apply measures to reduce investment to manageable levels and to prevent costly duplication by coordinating expenditures of competing communes or republics for expensive foreign engineering or other technical assistance. There is also a tendency to start large enterprises rather than small ones, a tendency which the Investment Bank has tried to discourage when financial and managerial resources were not up to the aspirations of the sponsors.

Although the Investment Bank has made some grants on behalf of the Federation from special funds transferred from the federal budget for highway, railway, port, airport and land reclamation projects, almost all its transactions are in the form of repayable loans. For some especially desirable social or economic purposes designated by the Federation, e.g., for projects in the less developed regions of the country or for those which promise to improve the balance of payments, the Bank has made loans from earmarked resources of the General Investment Fund, when satisfied with the applicant's financial status and the economic soundness of the project. Usually, however, loans from the General Investment Fund have been made on the basis of competitive bidding, since the amounts applied for generally exceed available funds.

When the federal plans provide for expanding specific sectors, the Investment Bank announces in the Official Gazette its willingness to make loans for appropriate projects and the conditions on which it is prepared to make the loans. An applicant for a loan (which may be an economic organization, or a republican or local government) is required to submit detailed economic and technical documentation on the project and on the applicant's ability to carry it out. Information to be furnished includes an estimate of the period of construction, the expected profit to be realized from the operation of the completed project, construction costs per unit of capacity and per unit of output, foreign exchange requirements, engineering designs, equipment specifications, the applicant's total investment program, its financial position and as to how it plans to meet the Bank's conditions for the loan.

While studying applications, the Bank consults with the appropriate chambers, associations and other interested groups. The screening process for small loans may require only a month or two, but the fact that the Bank takes up to a year before making decisions on larger loans has brought some criticism. On the other hand, some delays have undoubtedly been due to incomplete or otherwise inadequate documentation submitted by would-be borrowers. Some progress has been made in improving the quality of project documentation, but there is room for further improvement. There is little question, however, that the system of approving projects now in effect is considerably more efficient than the one which prevailed before 1954, when projects were frequently approved without adequate preliminary economic and technical studies.

If, after screening the applications, the Bank is satisfied that more than one applicant is qualified to carry out the project and service the loan, it will generally apply a series of economic criteria to determine to which applicant to make the loan. These criteria include expected profits from the project, investment outlay per unit of capacity, time required to complete the project, repayment prospects, proportion of finance for the project from the applicant's own resources and rate of interest offered by the borrower. When selecting a project for a loan, the Bank tries to eliminate political factors. In an attempt to use economic criteria even when giving preference to less developed areas, the Bank may separate the competitive bidding for projects in depressed areas from those in the more advanced areas. The Bank may also require that the borrower engage consultants, reorganize, improve the management or otherwise take steps to make an enterprise more efficient before it will make a loan.

The procedure followed in distributing investment resources represents an attempt on the part of the Investment Bank to approximate the effects of a free market for investment funds. To the extent that this objective can be realized, the system of competitive bidding for investment loans is superior to the old system of allocation solely by administrative means. On the other hand, the application of the criteria must be extremely difficult. A few years ago, the rate of interest to be paid and the expected profitability of the project were given the greatest weight; more recently, the proportion of expected additional output to the proposed investment and the effect of potential foreign exchange earnings on the balance of payments have become the most important considerations. It is also doubtful whether a meaningful calculation of profitability is possible in view of the prevailing method of setting wages and salaries and the distortions in the country's price structure. Moreover, there are projects which are only indirectly productive for which it is not possible to determine the rate of return with any reasonable degree of accuracy.

In addition to the use of the enumerated criteria, preference for investments in some economic sectors over others is imposed by regulations which set minima for participation by borrowers in the financing of projects for which the Bank makes loans. The minimum extent to which a borrower is required to participate in financing a project is fixed between 5 and 80 percent, depending on the importance which the federal plan assigns to the various sectors. Participation by the borrower in financing the project is considered important by the authorities, not only because it stimulates the borrower's interest in the efficient and rapid completion of the project, but also because it helps to channel local resources toward achieving the goals of the federal plans. Economic chambers, the unions and republics, all of which favor further decentralization of investment, have been trying to persuade the central authorities to eliminate, or at least reduce, the requirement for borrower participation in projects financed by the Investment Bank. Opponents of the requirement contend that federal attempts to channel investments through participation by borrowers may be diverting local funds from the most economic investments when localities give up high-yielding local projects in order to obtain additional funds from the Investment Bank for projects, with lower yields, favored by the central authorities.

The agreement which the Bank concludes with its borrowers spells out in detail the obligations of both parties. If the cost of the project should turn out to be higher than estimated, the increased cost must generally be borne by the borrower. To cover this contingency, to serve as security for partial repayment of the loan and to provide a contingency in case the cost of the project is higher than estimated, the borrower is required to make a guarantee deposit with the Investment Bank, usually equal to 5 percent, or exceptionally 10 percent, of the loan. As might be expected, this requirement has resulted in better estimation of costs by applicants and quicker and more rational execution of projects, "but in spite of this improvement, in some cases there is still a problem of achieving cheaper, faster implementation of investment projects."[32]

The Investment Bank may also require a loan to an economic organization to be guaranteed by the commune or district in which the borrower operates. While the interest rate may be determined by competitive bidding, in specific sectors which the federal plan wishes to stimulate, it is prescribed by the Investment Bank, sometimes at 6 percent, usually at a rate between 2 and 4 percent per annum, and in some cases at a rate of only 0.5 percent or 1 percent. The Bank makes loans for periods which extend to 30 years, although for electric power they may be for as much as 50 years. Since in most cases, the making of a loan depends partly on the

32. Papic, Augustin. *The Yugoslav Investment Bank.* [Washington, EDI, IBRD], 1957 (Mimeographed).

speed of repayment, the average life of loans made by the Investment Bank is much shorter. In 1958, the average period of all loans to industry was eight years.[33]

The Federation's share of investment accounted for four-fifths of the total in 1952,[34] but declined rapidly thereafter with the progress of decentralization. In terms of ownership of investment funds in recent years, about 33 to 35 percent of the total is estimated to belong to the General Investment Fund, approximately 35 percent to the investment funds of republics and local governments and about 30 to 32 percent to the funds of enterprises.[35] The decentralization of investment holdings appears to be continuing. The Draft Federal Social Plan for 1962 estimates that 71 percent of available investment funds belong to the various economic organizations, republics, local governments and autonomous agencies.

The Federation nevertheless has exercised much more control than these figures might indicate over both the amounts and ways in which other governmental units and enterprises spend from their investment funds. In the first place, the annual federal plans or other federal regulations fix ceilings on the proportions of their investment funds which republics, local authorities and enterprises may spend during each annual plan period either as an anti-inflationary measure or to prevent enterprises from spending more than they earn. Usually, only funds accumulated prior to the current year can be spent; current receipts are generally immobilized in the year received. For example, 70 percent of the current income of enterprises in 1961, after payment of taxes and wages, was blocked until 1962. In addition, the remaining 30 percent of current net income could be used only as working capital.

Secondly, the Investment Bank's requirement that borrowers and guarantors contribute a portion of their own investment resources toward financing projects for which the Bank lends has made it

33. Papic, Augustin. "Investment Financing in Yugoslavia," in "Collective Economy in Yugoslavia," p. 224.

34. "Yugoslavia's Social Plan and Its Application," in *Review of International Affairs* (Beograd), February 13, 1952, p. 14.

35. Jelic, Bora. "The Yugoslav Economic System—Institutional Framework and Functioning," in "Collective Economy in Yugoslavia," p. 104.

possible for the Bank recently to direct from two-thirds to four-fifths of the total investment in the country toward achieving the objectives in the federal plans. This centralized control over most investment, as well as over short-term credit, has constituted an effective means for assuring that decentralized holdings of investment resources are utilized in the main in accordance with the objectives of the federal plans.

There are, however, cases in which enterprises and communes initiate projects in sectors in which the federal plan does not provide for expansion, if their own resources permit them to carry out the projects.[36] There is no way of telling how much local investment has deviated from the objectives of the plans. One foreign observer[37] estimated that it amounts to 10 percent of total investment. Although investments which do not coincide with plan objectives appear to be of substantial size, the authorities are prepared to accept these deviations from the federal plans as the price for preserving and fostering local initiative and to maximize incomes.

The foreign trade reforms of 1961 which followed increases in subsidized rents and prices for public utility services in 1960

36. *The New York Times* of August 21, 1960, carried the following story:

"There are many local-industry success stories, such as that of the ten-man tailoring workshop set up several years ago by the town of Bijeljina, the center of a farming area on the Drina River south and west of Belgrade. Today this enterprise is a full-fledged factory employing 1,500 people.

"But the most interesting of these stories—because it illustrates the degree to which individual initiative can play a role even in a Communist society—concerns a cosmetics plant in Leskovac, a small textile center in backward South Serbia.

"Before World War II, a pharmacist in the town made a little extra money preparing face creams. When the war ended he was old, his shop was nationalized and he was retired.

"But he was not happy. He wanted to work and he finally persuaded the town officials to help him set up a little enterprise to make those same face creams. The officials got him one room and two helpers and told him to go ahead.

"The old man is now dead, but the enterprise he fought to establish has a brand new factory, all the money for which came from its own funds. It has ninety employees and all the business it can handle."

37. Neuberger, Egon. *Central Banking in Semi-Planned Economies: Yugoslav Case.* Unpublished Ph.D. thesis, Harvard University, Cambridge, Mass., 1957, p. 187.

promise to reduce price distortions sufficiently to make possible greater reliance on market forces to guide investment. As a consequence, new measures were introduced in 1961 which should result in further decentralization of both investment decisions and financing. Resources of the General Investment Fund are to be largely earmarked for major investment projects. Central allocation of investment funds from the General Investment Fund will hereafter be limited to a few large-scale projects for infrastructure and to projects required to correct structural unbalances. In order to assure more rapid development of economically backward areas of the country, investments from a special fund set up for this purpose, to be administered by the Investment and Agricultural Banks, will also be determined centrally. However, for the great number of smaller investment projects which make up the bulk of new investments, decision-making will be further decentralized. Most investment loans are to be made, not by the Investment Bank, as in the past, but by communal banks to which bank deposits of republics and local governments have been transferred. Communal banks are also to take over lending operations to enterprises formerly handled by the National Bank. The National Bank has sometimes been under strong pressure from interested groups to grant credits to enterprises for purposes whose merits the National Bank was not always in position to assess. Since the communal banks are located in the area in which enterprises applying for loans operate and draw on funds guaranteed by local economic organizations and institutions, they are expected to be in better position than the National Bank to gauge the creditworthiness of projects and applicants, as well as to withstand pressure for making uneconomic loans. Moreover, the communal banks are expected to have greater independence from local governments as the result of a new regulation which requires that two-thirds of their management be composed of representatives of economic organizations. The National Bank, through the control it exercises over (1) obligatory reserves which all other banks must deposit in the National Bank, (2) the volume of credit to banks within the limits of the credit ceilings fixed by the Federal Executive Council,

(3) interest rates, and (4) rules which banks must follow when making loans (none of which has hitherto played a decisive role in the banking and credit system), will still be in position to influence the lending policies of the communal banks. Nevertheless, the new measures should greatly enhance the importance of the communal banks as investment media, especially if they are permitted (as proposed) to absorb idle funds in their areas through the sale of bonds.

The new measures for decentralizing investment decisions were adopted because the authorities felt that the Investment Bank (which generally makes important investment decisions at its headquarters in Belgrade, even though equipped with 29 branches throughout the country), is not as favorably situated as the communal banks both to mobilize savings and to determine the merits of local investment opportunities for small projects which depend, ultimately, on the action of large numbers of enterprises reacting to local market situations. While the new approach promises to give economic organizations more liberty to choose investment projects and hence may lead to a more economic utilization of investment resources, it remains to be seen whether the necessity of reaching centrally set investment targets can be reconciled with considerably greater latitude at the local level to determine where, when and how much to invest. There is also the possibility that greater communal control over investment resources may lead to dispersion of "territorialization" of investment resources, so that they may not be available where needed.

The Investment Bank initiated a plan, in the latter part of 1958, for increasing its importance as Yugoslavia's most important "capital market" by seeking deposits from economic organizations and local government with idle investment funds. While the offer of a small interest payment on these deposits is not enough by itself to attract depositors, promises of preferential treatment for depositors' loan applications and a commitment to provide the foreign exchange resources required for importing capital equipment covered by such loans should provide the necessary incentives to attract a significant amount of deposits. If the plan is successful, it offers the Investment Bank an opportunity to counteract the tendency toward territorialization of investment resources, which the recent decentralization of control over local investment decisions may entail.

INVESTMENT: INVESTMENT OUTLAYS

Net investment in recent years on the basis of Yugoslav prices, has approximated 30 percent of net social product, calculated either by Yugoslav or Western standards. However, if Yugoslav prices are brought into line with world prices, the ratio of real investment to social product might be about 26 percent. These rates of investment are impressive, especially if account is taken of the high share of the national income which has gone for defense expenditures. In 1953, the proportion of the national income spent for defense was 16 percent. It declined each year, but in 1957 the proportion was still 9 percent. It has been lower since then. On the basis of net investment at 30 percent of social product, net investment financed by domestic savings accounted for 27 percent of social product and financing from abroad from 3 percent.

Yugoslavia's high levels of savings and investment have been achieved chiefly through taxation and reinvestment of large proportions of the profits of socialized enterprises. As seen earlier, the high level of savings is largely predetermined and assured by a planned system of income distribution in which the savings of enterprises are set aside first from their incomes, leaving consumption as a residual. This feature, central to the Yugoslav system of income distribution, is, of course, a reversal of the situation prevailing in most other countries. The foreign exchange system has favored industry over agriculture and brought about a shift in incomes from the largely private agricultural sector to socialized industry. This shift of incomes greatly facilitates the collection of substantial proportions of the national product in taxes and other contributions. Moreover, official policies which promote the accumulation and ploughing back of investment funds by socialized enterprises and the Investment Bank's requirement that borrowers repay loans in the shortest possible time also help induce a higher level of savings. Personal savings, although increasing, are still small. Most capital formation in Yugoslavia is publicly financed and private investment is almost entirely limited to agriculture and urban housing. Between 1952 and 1956, 89 percent of total investment was public and only about 11 percent was private.

ROLE OF ECONOMIC ORGANIZATIONS
(EXCLUDING ENTERPRISES)

After the abolition of the federal ministries, economic chambers gradually emerged as the most effective means for keeping economic organizations in line with the federal plans and for combating monopolistic practices and the excessive "localism" or "particularism" which attended decentralization. Although most economic organizations were already members of economic chambers, it was made mandatory in 1957 for all socialized economic organizations to belong to the appropriate chamber in each sector of the economy. Each economic chamber has the legal status of a self-managed economic organization and operates with a paid secretariat. The most important chamber, the Federal Chamber of Industry, is composed, not only of all industrial and mining enterprises, but also of 25 technical (or production) associations into which each branch of industry and mining is divided. There are also chambers for foreign trade, transport, construction, agriculture, etc.

The Federation has turned over to the economic chambers supervisory and coordinating powers formerly exercised by federal ministries or other state organs. The chambers make recommendations to their members on a wide range of matters affecting production, marketing and distribution of net income. These recommendations must in general be adopted by their members. The chambers are consulted by the Federal Planning Institute when the federal plans are drafted. Moreover, "in organizing the development of production and economic activities, the chambers always keep in sight the short-term and long-term economic plans . . . (and they) . . .

lend specific assistance to organizations in order to enable the general plans to be carried out."[38]

ROLE OF POLITICAL AND SOCIAL ORGANIZATIONS

Before decentralization, the Communist Party of Yugoslavia intervened directly as an organization in both the government and the economy. It set developmental policy, determined the means by which plans were to be implemented, and participated actively in carrying out the plans. The Party issued instructions which government and enterprises were expected to put into effect, but Party membership was so thoroughly interlocked with governmental leadership and enterprise management that the legal division of authority among them had more formal than practical significance.

At the end of 1952, the Party announced a shift in its role and, to emphasize the change, renamed itself the Communist League of Yugoslavia. Instead of relying on compulsion, the League saw itself as a force for political and ideological education of the 95 percent of the Yugoslavs who were not members of the League. In their capacity as Communists, members were no longer to interfere in the affairs of government or enterprises but were to rely on persuasion to influence decisions. By 1953, while most of the important positions in government, particularly in the Federation and in the Republics, continued to be filled by members of the League, there was a notable increase in the number of managers of enterprises who were not members. In 1953, only one-third of the members of workers' councils were members of the League; and if there were enterprises which were still dominated by League members, there were also enterprises which were not.

While the League of Communists, like its predecessor, plays a vital part in formulating economic development policy and in initiating important legislation, it now largely relies on the efforts of its members acting as individuals to convince economic organizations

38. Balog, Nikola. "Associations of Economic Organizations," in "Collective Economy in Yugoslavia," pp. 252-253.

to make decisions and to take actions which are consistent with objectives of the federal plans. Members of the League in enterprises may not, by virtue of their political affiliation, singly or as a group, impose their will on management; instead, they must endeavor to persuade the majority to conform to the objectives of the plans and to support their views by argument and personal example. "The basic working method is persuasion."[39]

The League of Communists also works through a large number of organizations to influence public opinion and decision-making at different levels. The most important of these, numerically as well as otherwise, is the Socialist Alliance of the Working People of Yugoslavia with a membership in 1959 of almost 6 million divided into almost 23,500 basic groups. The Socialist Alliance is an organization established for political education of the people, but it also participates actively in politics and it normally is the means by which candidates for political office are nominated. As in the case of the Confederation of Trade Unions, most of the officers of the Socialist Alliance are also leaders of the League of Communists, although most members of the trade unions or the Socialist Alliance are not. The League of Communists also endeavors to obtain social and political understanding and voluntary compliance with plan objectives through its members' active participation in women's, children's and youth organizations; veterans, scientific, cultural, artistic, technical, sporting and other associations, societies of professionals, etc.

Yugoslav officials have let it be known that the new Constitution to go into effect in 1962 will reduce further the powers of local League of Communist organizations while increasing those of the Socialist Alliance. Moreover, the new Constitution will also introduce the principle of rotation of office for elected officials. By prohibiting re-election of officials immediately after they have completed their first term of office, the authorities hope to "guard against the establishment of a permanent bureaucracy."[40] These changes, while likely to widen popular participation in political

39. "Political and Social Organizations in Yugoslavia," *Statistical Pocket Book of Yugoslavia,* Federal Statistical Institute, Beograd, 1960, p. 202.
40. *The New York Times,* February 22, 1961.

activity, will not necessarily involve real relaxation of the League's control since officers of the League, through "a system of inter-locking directorates," still hold most of the important offices in the government, the Social Alliance, the trade unions and most other influential organizations.

RESULTS OBTAINED

After four years of stagnation between 1949 and 1952, when the national income increased by less than 2 percent annually, the Yugoslav economy has grown at a striking pace. Aided by the high level of investment, more efficient use of capital made possible by progressive decentralization of economic decision-making and the strengthening of market forces and an increasing supply of consumer goods of improved quality which stimulated greater effort, real output expanded by an average of over 10 percent annually after 1952. Moreover, the rate of growth of the national income has been accelerating. From 1953 to 1956, the increase averaged 8.4 percent; in the period 1957-60, it rose to the phenomenal level of 12.9 percent annually.[41]

However, in 1961 the rate of growth fell to about 5.5 percent, the lowest in a decade, because a severe drought reduced harvests and less than planned increases in industrial production, as well as stagnation in the level of exports, followed foreign exchange and other reforms in that year. Government officials profess no great concern about this slowdown, which they consider to be due to transitory factors. On the other hand, there are indications that Yugoslavia may have reached a point in its development at which, at least in the short run, rates of growth are likely to be less spectacular than in recent years.

As a consequence of continued intensive industrialization, the relative standing of the manufacturing-mining and agricultural sectors in gross social product has been reversed. The contribution of manufacturing–mining rose from about 25 percent of gross

41. A Summary of the Draft of the Social Plan for Economic Development of Yugoslavia for the Period 1961 to 1965. Translation (Mimeographed).

social product in 1939 to 41 percent in 1959. In spite of a large rise in agricultural production, the share of agriculture and forestry in social product dropped from 44 percent in 1939 to only 30 percent in 1959.

Yugoslav investment from 1952 continued to stress industrialization and more than half of present manufacturing capacity came into production after that year. Not only new products, but new branches of industry, have been created which did not exist in 1952. Industrial output increased by an average of over 13 percent between 1952 and 1959. It averaged 12.8 percent annually in 1953-56 and rose to 14.2 percent in 1957-60. Industrial production in 1960 was 4.5 times greater than in 1939. In contrast with previous years when output of heavy industry products expanded more rapidly than output in other branches of industry, production of industrial materials and consumer goods expanded at about the same rate as the output of capital goods in recent years.

The change in official attitude toward agriculture and the improvement in agricultural terms of trade has been accomplished by successes in increasing output. Between 1953 and 1956, agricultural production grew by only 4.1 percent annually, but, between 1957 and 1959, the annual increase averaged 10.5 percent. Harvests in 1960 and 1961, however, were well below levels called for in the plans for those years and agricultural output planned for 1962 is only 5 percent higher than it was in 1959. While adverse weather conditions were partly responsible for the poor showing in the last two years, there is also evidence that Yugoslav agriculture has yet to devise ways of introducing advanced technology and to overcome inefficiencies inherent in the operation of the large number of small individual holdings which comprise nine-tenths of the country's arable land. It may well be, also, that economic incentives to farmers are still inadequate to call forward the necessary effort to increase output sufficiently.

Personal consumption as a proportion of national income has been severely restricted by the high investment ratio, but there has nevertheless been a marked improvement in consumption because of the rise in national income and an increase in real incomes. Real personal consumption grew by an average of 3.2 percent between 1953 and 1956 and rose to 9.9 percent between 1957 and 1960. It is estimated that personal consumption and the social standard (housing, health and other welfare services) together have increased at a rate equal to the rate of increase in the national income in recent years.[42]

Between 1953 and 1959, the gainfully employed in agriculture declined from about two-thirds of the labor force to just over one-half; in the same years, the proportion of the labor force employed in industry and mining increased from 7 to 12 percent of the total. Although labor productivity has increased both in industry and agriculture in the past eight years at an impressive average rate of about 8.8 percent annually, low productivity and a lack of skilled workers, managers and technicians, probably represent the greatest impediments to further economic growth in the short run, especially in socialized industry.

The foreign exchange reform, the steps taken to turn over to the communal banks larger responsibilities for extending credit and the considerable enlargement of the share of enterprise incomes which workers' councils will be allowed to distribute, these reflect the official view that in 1961, "conditions are ripe for widening the system of self-management in sectors where it is not yet completely built up, for doing away with administrative intervention where it is no longer necessary and where it impedes successful development of the economy and of social relations."[43] Since the effect of these changes will be to permit the market to operate more freely and "to confirm still more strongly the principle of remuneration according to work,"[44] the management of enterprises and the operation of the economy promise, if anything, to be smoother and more efficient than in the past.

42. Todorovic, Mijalko. *Current Problems of Economic Policy*. Beograd, Jugoslavija, 1959, p. 9.

43. Jelic, Borivoje. "The Federal Social Plan for 1961," *Review of International Affairs* (Beograd), Vol. 12, No. 259, January 20, 1961, p. 12.

44. *Ibid.*

VII.

SUMMARY AND CONCLUSIONS

THE FOREGOING ACCOUNT indicates the variety of means by which the federal plans are carried out. The state makes the important decisions and enunciates the basic objectives and targets in the federal plans, as well as the instruments of economic policy by which they are implemented. Thereby it shapes the institutional framework within which the economy operates. These instruments are embodied in various but related forms in the methods (a) by which the workers are remunerated, (b) by which the enterprise and governmental investment funds are distributed, (c) of granting short-term credits and financing investments, of governmental budgets, of taxation, of pricing and for conducting foreign trade.

Although the state has the legal power and means to intervene directly to carry out its objectives, and on some occasions does so, it has chosen as a matter of policy to rely increasingly on indirect financial and fiscal instruments to realize the objectives of the federal plans. It retains control over production, the distribution of income, investment and consumption largely through the system of taxation and contributions by enterprises, through the allocation of investment and foreign exchange resources, by influencing the supply and direction of credit, and to a diminishing extent, by the setting of price ceilings and restrictions on foreign exchange and trade. It determines the amount of savings and consequently the resources available for consumption in the community by varying the rates of interest paid by enterprises on capital, the turnover and other retail taxes, personal income taxes, the tax on enterprise

88

profits and the proportion used for investment, the rates and conditions under which enterprises charge depreciation and, finally, by
deciding how much of the receipts on all levels of government and
enterprise shall be invested in the economy.

In addition, it relies on a comprehensive network of trade unions,
trade associations and economic chambers, as well as on the communes, to guide and coordinate local economic activities with national objectives and on a variety of political organizations to
inform and persuade the people to cooperate with the aims of the
plans. The immediate objectives of some of these entities may
differ from one another and from those of the Federation. Thus,
the trade unions try to see that the wage scale of a specific economic organization corresponds to actual productive efficiency on
all working levels. The technical association or economic chamber
may be more concerned to assure that salary schedules in similar
enterprises operating in the same branch or sector of the economy
are consistent. The commune, which has relied on taxes on personal income for substantial revenues, has often successfully forced
an enterprise in its territory to increase unduly workers' earnings
or to employ more workers than required, while the federation is
more concerned to see, among other things, that enterprises distribute earnings in conformity with the goals of the federal plans
and that they contribute enough of their income to fulfill the investment targets of the plans.

These objectives are not necessarily contradictory. Frequently,
they are not but they may be at times. Thus, in 1954, taxes levied
by republics and local authorities were so high that they reduced
unduly the ability of enterprises to pay necessary incentive wages
and to invest adequately. However, when the prevailing instruments of economic policy induce behavior or yield results which
are too far out of line with general objectives, or the situation
changes, the instruments are soon adjusted. Thus, to counteract
what was considered an undue interest on the part of the communes
in maximizing wage and salary distributions (to the detriment of
investment), the new regulations in 1961 provided for a new tax
for the benefit of communes and republics on sums allocated by
enterprises to their investment funds.

At times there are also important differences in point of view about the extent to which the state should intervene in economic activity. Thus, the more developed regions and more efficient enterprises tend to favor further decentralization and greater reliance on the market, while the less developed regions of the country and enterprises, which find it difficult to compete, prefer more centralized control. Attempts to reconcile these opposing points of view have sometimes caused policy to oscillate back and forth, but the general trend, especially in recent years, has been toward greater decentralization of responsibility for economic decision-making and increased reliance on market forces — always, of course, within the limits of the prevailing political system.

In general, the system of "checks and balances" formed by the complex of economic chambers, associations and trade unions, and the authorities of local, regional, republican and Federation governments, in which each is assigned specific tasks for implementing the plans, works well. Within the framework of a single economic, social and political philosophy, which has the effect of orienting all entities toward the Federation's point of view, the objectives of each entity manage to be reconciled to conform generally with federal planning goals without unduly undermining the essential autonomy of economic organizations. This reconciliation of activities and objectives is, of course, aided by a cadre of leaders from the League of Communists whose influence, whether as individuals or as a group, is felt at all levels of economic and social activity.

An important contributing factor in accounting for the high rate of economic growth is the systematic way in which the Yugoslavs have imported from any available source and have applied advanced techniques and knowledge. This has, in turn, been aided by an educational structure which seeks out and educates promising young people who can utilize advanced procedures. Investment in education and training is built into Yugoslav plans, with a fixed charge on enterprises as a contribution for these purposes.

Economic activity is conducted in an atmosphere which emphasizes the widest participation of the populace in self-management of enterprises, organizations and local government reflecting the

Federation's pragmatic recognition of the role of economic incentives in getting people to do voluntarily what they would resist doing under compulsion. The economic and social structure which has evolved in the past decade is now so thoroughly committed on all sides to further decentralization of economic decision-making, that the trend may well be irreversible. This causes no concern to the authorities, whose avowed policy is to place ever-increasing reliance on the market. In November 1960, when the President of Yugoslavia announced that as a consequence of recent progress, a new constitution would be adopted in 1962, he stated that it would establish the worker as the "producer and manager, while the state should appear only as a factor of coordination."[45]

45. *The New York Times,* February 11, 1961.

Appendix A

THE FIVE-YEAR PLAN FOR 1947-51

THE PLAN provided that new investments during the five years were to be 278.3 billion dinars (US$5.6 billion on the basis of an exchange rate of 50 dinars to US$1.00) at 1947 prices, or about 28 percent of the total estimated national income during the entire period. The Plan gave primary emphasis to industry, mining and electric power, allotting 41.5 percent of total planned investment to these sectors. It also provided substantially for transportation and communications with 26.1 percent of total investment and for social investments (housing, public services, health and education) with 20 percent of the total; in contrast, it allocated only 8.3 percent to agriculture and forestry.

In order to equalize economic development throughout the country, proportionately greater investments were to be allocated to the less developed republics than to the more developed. Thus, investments in Serbia, Croatia and Slovenia were scheduled in 1951 to be about four times greater than in 1939, but in Bosnia and Herzogovina, Macedonia and Montenegro they were to be seven or eight times greater than the prewar level. The Plan estimated that industrial production in 1951 would respond to these differing rates of investment by expanding ten times over 1939 in Bosnia and Herzogovina and 26 times in Macedonia, while output in the three more developed republics would increase by only about four times over the same period.

The national income in 1951 was expected to rise to about double the prewar level. The greatest increase was to be registered in industrial output which would increase by 1951 to almost five times the 1939 level. This would bring about an increase in the share of industry in the total national income from less than 19 percent in 1939 to over 49 percent in 1951.

Within the industrial sector, the aim was to achieve self-sufficiency as rapidly as possible in capital goods, the output of which in 1951 was to be 6.5 times greater than in 1939. While the production of manufactured consumption goods was not to increase quite as much as capital goods output, it was nevertheless scheduled to increase by four times. Before the war, capital goods had accounted for 43 percent of total industrial production and consumption goods for 57 percent; because of the greater projected rate of growth for capital goods, however, the prewar position was expected to be exactly reversed in 1951, with capital goods production amounting to 57 percent and consumer goods to 43 percent of total industrial production. By 1951, many products never before manufactured in Yugoslavia were to be produced, including trucks, tractors, heavy machine tools, electrical and agricultural machinery, synthetic rubber and fibers, fertilizers, bicycles, typewriters and radios.

In order to bring about the desired increase in industrial output, the Plan envisaged the erection of the most modern factories, which would take advantage of the latest innovations of science and technology in using and conserving fuels and in using the most advanced mass-production techniques. Industrial waste from large plants, such as metal shavings, leather, cotton and rubber waste, bristles, feathers, etc., were to be salvaged for the use of artisans, whose output in 1951 was expected to be 50 percent higher than in 1939.

Agricultural production was also expected to rise, but the targets for this sector were much more modest than for industry. The Plan called for only a 20 percent increase by 1951 to reach prewar levels for basic food crops (breadgrains, fats, meats, milk, etc.) and a shift to industrial crops (sugar beets, tobacco, cotton and other textile fibers). It was expected that output of industrial crops would be much higher than output of food crops, thereby raising total agricultural production in 1951 to a point about 52 percent above the 1939 level.

Investments in agriculture and forestry were to be used for tractors and farm machinery, fertilizers, drainage, irrigation and reforestation. However, most of the increased agricultural output was to be obtained through higher yields per unit of land (acreage sown was to be increased by only 6 percent) improved agricultural techniques and greater use of fertilizers and equipment. The quality and yield of cattle and hogs were also to benefit from improved veterinarian facilities and pharmaceutical supplies, better husbandry and widespread use of artificial insemination.

The different rates of expansion in output for industry and agriculture were expected to reverse the relative importance of each sector. In 1939, industrial production had contributed 45 percent of combined output and agriculture 55 percent; in 1951, industry's contribution would amount to 64 percent of combined output while agriculture would account for only 36 percent.

The Plan also provided for the restoration and expansion of transportation and communication facilities damaged during the war. The length of railroad lines was to be increased by more than 2,000 kilometers, the tonnage of the merchant marine was to be increased by more than half and inland water transport was also to expand beyond prewar levels. The number of airplanes in 1951 was to be five times greater than before the war and ten new airports were to be built. More than 600 kilometers of new highway with high specifications were to be constructed and large-scale repairs on an additional 10,000 kilometers of highway were to be carried out; 700 meters of new bridges were to be built and a total of 13,450 meters of existing steel or concrete bridges were to be reconstructed. The number of buses, trucks, trailers and passenger cars was to be greatly increased and new garages and repair facilities constructed to care for them. In order to improve communication facilities, 20,880 kilometers of new telephone and telegraph lines were to be added, 275 automatic telephone exchanges and 625 teleprinters were to be installed, and 656 general post offices and 1,450 branch post offices were to be opened.

Although the rate of investment was to be much higher than before, consumption standards and social services were nevertheless to rise. By 1951, the average person was to receive 113 percent more fats, 215 percent more oil, 111 percent more fish and meat, 200 percent more sugar, 120 percent more textiles and 200 percent more shoes than in 1939. The amount of available food was also to be increased through the erection of many food storage and processing plants for conserving suppliers. Trading methods were to be improved until, in 1951, trade was to be 80 percent higher than prewar and trading costs would average only 10 percent of retail prices. Through the use of mass-produced prefabricated houses, the equivalent of about 200,000 new family units was to be built and ready for occupancy when the plan period ended. Investment in facilities for improving the health of the people were also to be substantial. 110 new hospitals with 14,300 beds would be built as well as 730 dispensaries and clinics. Nor were sports facilities to be forgotten, the Plan providing that 900 million dinars (US$18 million) were to be disbursed "for the building of various sports premises and for the purchase of material indispensable for the development of physical culture."

In education, the objective was "to raise the general cultural level of the people, completely stamp out illiteracy [estimated at 20 percent of the population], provide elementary schooling for all children of school age . . ." and to provide seven years' schooling for 60 percent of the children. To accomplish these tasks, the Plan called for investment of 5.9 billion dinars (US$118 million) and the construction of one million square meters of schools. In addition, new theaters, museums, galleries, a film center near Belgrade, and new radio broadcasting stations were to be erected throughout the nation to raise the cultural level of the people.

The Plan also provided for the establishment of special training courses to increase the number of skilled workers from 350,000 to 750,000 by 1951, the number of workers with secondary school training from 65,000 to 150,000, and the number of university-trained personnel to 5,000. The authorities believed that the combined effects of improved efficiency they considered inherent in centralized planning, a hard working and honest corps of administrators and the ploughing back of profits would make it possible to develop Yugoslavia's largely untapped, natural resources at unprecedented rates.

Appendix B

ORGANIZATION OF THE FEDERAL PLANNING INSTITUTE

THERE ARE 13 technical divisions in the Federal Planning Institute and one administrative division. As indicated in the chart which follows, 12 of the technical divisions are evenly divided into two main groups: (1) "Balancing" and (2) "Production and Trade." The work done by these divisions is apparent from their titles. The thirteenth technical unit, the Division for Economic Research and Planning Methodology, is mostly concerned with evolving and perfecting planning techniques. Recently, it has worked on problems associated with the determination of the optimum rate of investment, the practical application of input-output analysis in planning and the preparation of models of economic development.

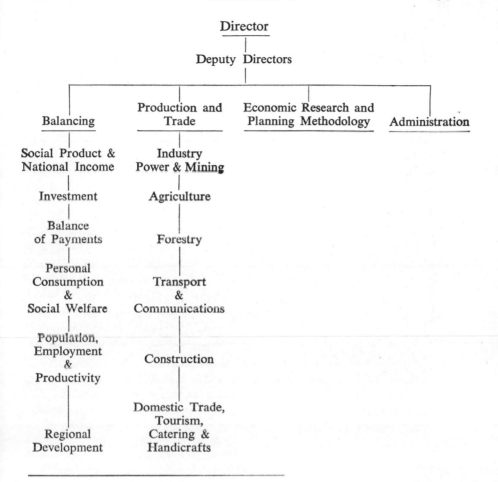

Director

Deputy Directors

| Balancing | Production and Trade | Economic Research and Planning Methodology | Administration |

Balancing:
- Social Product & National Income
- Investment
- Balance of Payments
- Personal Consumption & Social Welfare
- Population, Employment & Productivity
- Regional Development

Production and Trade:
- Industry Power & Mining
- Agriculture
- Forestry
- Transport & Communications
- Construction
- Domestic Trade, Tourism, Catering & Handicrafts

SOURCE: Adapted from Kubovic, B. and Trickovic, V., *National and Regional Economic Planning in Yugoslavia,* Beograd, 1961, Chart 2 following text.

Appendix C

THE FEDERAL SOCIAL PLAN FOR 1957-61

As INDICATED in the text, the Plan had four main parts: Part One contained a brief account of (a) the problems which the economy faced — shortages of electric power and raw materials, insufficient expansion of agricultural output and other production for consumption and the deficit in the balance of payments, (b) the potentialities for further growth as a consequence of the building up of industrial and other capacity in previous years and (c) the plan's basic objectives — to ensure regular and faster growth of the national income and total production, especially in agriculture; to reduce the balance of payments deficit by increasing exports, to bring about a steady improvement in the standard of living; consistent with these objectives, to aid the development of the country's economically underdeveloped areas and finally, by economic development to expand and strengthen the system of workers' management in economic organizations and local self-government.

Part Two of the Plan estimated that the gross social product would increase by 57.6 percent between 1956 and 1961, with an average annual rise of 9.5 percent; the national income would increase by 54.4 percent in the same period, or 9.1 percent annually. These estimates were based on the following expected increases in sectoral output:

Sector	Percentage (1961) Increase (1956)	Average annual increase: percent
Industry	70.0	11.0
Agriculture	41.2	7.4
Forestry	8.4	0.6
Construction	67.3	10.9
Transport	54.3	9.1
Commerce, Hotel Industry and Tourism	41.1	7.1
Handicrafts	43.2	7.4

It was estimated that these increases would permit an expansion of 69.2 percent in exports between 1956 and 1961, a rate well in excess of the anticipated rise in production, while imports would rise by only 42.0 percent, a rate of increase below that of gross social product. These changes made it possible to foresee a notable reduction in the balance of payments deficit during the five years.

As a consequence of these changes, the Plan envisioned that available resources, which were expected to rise by 53.3 percent (8.9 percent annually) taking foreign contributions into account, would permit personal consumption expenditures to increase by 41.9 percent (7.3 percent annually), housing and community services by 72.5 percent (11.5 percent per annum), making possible an accelerated improvement in real incomes of 40 to 45 percent or 7 to 8 percent each year.

The Plan also advocated that measures be taken to bring about an increase of total investments by 39.8 percent during the period. Excess industrial capacity which existed as a result of high investments in preceding years, new investments which would lead to quick returns and greater efficiency in construction, made it possible to reduce the pace of industrial investments without jeopardizing increased output. Social investments in housing, schools and other community services, which had lagged in previous years, were to increase much more (by 71.1 percent or 11.5 percent per annum) than economic investments in fixed and working capital (which were to increase 33.4 percent or 5.9 percent per annum).

Among investments in the economy, the highest priority was to be given to agriculture, in which investments were scheduled to rise by 195 percent. It was hoped in this way to increase output for exports, reduce imports and bring about a better supply of food products for the internal market and more raw materials for industry. By increasing agricultural exports and reducing such imports, the balance of payments deficit was to be reduced. Industrial investments, which had been favored before 1956, would rise during the entire period by only 11.9 percent. Those branches of industry which supported agriculture (processing of farm products, artificial fertilizer production, farm machine factories, etc.), or which had an export potential (including tourism) or which produced import substitutes, were to be encouraged, while heavy industry, which had been favored previously, was to have a low priority.

The Plan also provided, that in addition to investments made with their own funds, special help in the form of federal funds would be made available to the less developed regions of the country. The Plan also gave estimates of changes to be expected in employment, the composition of the nation's labor force and growth of labor productivity (which was expected to grow by 6 to 7 percent annually) through fuller utilization of existing capacities and improvement in labor skills.

Appendix D

THE FEDERAL SOCIAL PLAN FOR 1961-65

MORE THAN PREVIOUSLY, the Federal Social Plan for 1961-65 proposed to coordinate the Yugoslav economy with the international market. Investment during the 1961-65 period was to be concentrated on increasing production of commodities, which could be made from Yugoslav materials, for which there was either a ready market abroad or which could not easily be imported.

The Plan envisaged a yearly rise of 11.4 percent in gross social product and 11.2 percent in the national income, 13 percent in industrial output, 7.2 percent in agricultural production and 13.3 percent in construction, 11 percent in transport and 12.2 percent in trade. The volume of exports was to be increased annually by 13.8 percent and the volume of imports by 9.8 percent. The deficit on current account was to be eliminated and foreign exchange reserves built up, by increasing investments in industries with export potential, including tourism, and in those producing import substitutes. Special attention would be given to industries which consumed domestic raw materials. No major changes were to be made in the general pattern of investment, but investment was to rise slightly to 32.3 percent of gross social product as compared to 30.9 percent during the previous four years. Foreign participation in investment was to decline, from 5.5 percent of gross social product in 1960 to 3.7 percent in 1965.

Whereas the provisions in the second Five-Year Social Plan concentrated on cereal crops in order to obtain the greatest possible increase in the shortest time, the 1961-65 Plan provided for more balanced production, by putting greater emphasis on meat production, industrial crops, fruits and vegetables as well as cereals. It also provided for a large increase in domestic processing of agricultural products for exports. The socialized sector was expected to produce the major portion of the increase, while private farmers were expected to make major contributions to increases in output only for sugar beets and meat.

100

Appendix E

THE INSTRUMENTS OF ECONOMIC POLICY

THE DISTRIBUTION of gross receipts of economic organizations, according to the 1961 regulations, is shown in the chart on the following page. The Roman numerals which appear in parentheses in the text below refer to those on the chart.

The 1961 regulations divide the gross receipts of the economic organizations (I) into four main categories: costs of operation (II); turnover tax (VII); Ricardian rent (VIII) and the income of the enterprise (IX).

Costs of operation (II) are divided in turn into: cost of materials and services (III); a depreciation charge on fixed assets (IV); interest on capital assets (V) and miscellaneous contributions and membership fees (VI).

Material costs (III) include the value of materials and services used in production or distribution, as well as interest on loans. Depreciation (IV), is fixed as a percentage, based on the projected life of the assets. It is usually 5 or 6 percent, but sometimes as low as 4 percent, of the value of the fixed assets (machinery, buildings, transport equipment, etc.). Depreciation funds can now be used to replace fixed assets, for working capital or for debt service on loans contracted to purchase fixed assets. Each enterprise also pays a tax, called interest (V), on its aggregate assets (fixed and working). In principle, the charge amounts to 6 percent of the book value of the assets, but where the Federation wishes to stimulate the growth of an industry or where profits of an enterprise are low, it may be smaller or nothing. Thus, mines and steel mills pay 4 percent; transport, food distribution, tourism, catering and certain other industries pay 2 percent; electric power companies and certain other groups of enterprises pay 1 percent, while certain agricultural processing plants and others are partially or completely exempt from the tax. The proceeds of the tax on assets goes into the federal investment fund, except for a tax on assets of tourism and catering concerns, not exceeding 6 percent of the value of their assets, which

APPENDIX E

DISTRIBUTION OF GROSS RECEIPTS OF ECONOMIC ORGANIZATIONS

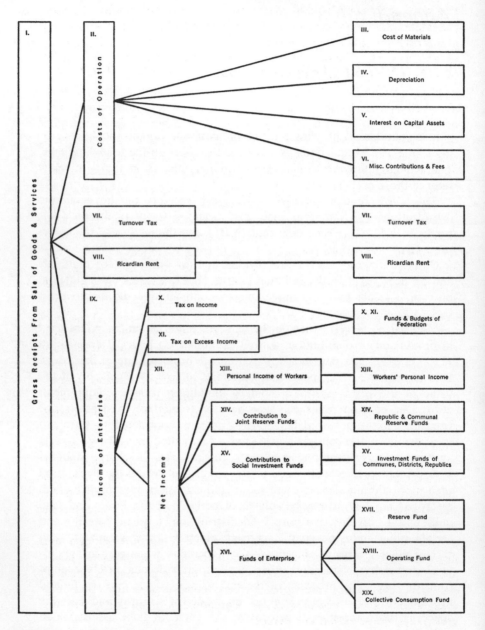

Source: Privredni Pregled (Economic Review), Beograd, March 6, 1961

communes may levy. The enterprise also pays, as a part of its operating costs, contributions and membership fees to associations of enterprises and chambers of commerce or industry (VI). It must also make a contribution equal to 1 percent of its wage bill for training workers, as well as certain additional social security payments when the record of illness in an enterprise is abnormally high.

The remainder, or "net income of the enterprise" (XII), is then allocated by the workers' council of an enterprise to wages and salaries or to the various funds of the enterprise. In distributing the net income of the enterprise, the enterprise is obligated to behave like a "good entrepreneur." An enterprise behaves like a good entrepreneur when it provides adequately for its investment needs and when the amounts distributed as wages are in accordance with the efforts of its labor force and are not due to market or other external factors, over which the enterprise had no control. In setting up criteria for distributing income, each enterprise must also take into account its own performance in relation to the performance and conditions of operation of other enterprises.

From the personal income of workers and employees (XIII), a tax of 13.5 percent was formerly withheld at the source. Beginning in 1961, this tax was consolidated with the school tax and increased to 15 percent. Communes may levy additional tax on personal incomes, but it may not exceed 1.5 percent of wages and salaries paid. A social security tax equal to 22 percent of personal income for most workers (20 percent for agricultural workers) is also deducted when wages and salaries are paid. In 1961, an additional 2 percent of personal incomes was also withheld as a social security surtax. (Prior to 1961, the social security tax was 45 percent of minimum, or "normal," salaries; the 1961 contributions are based on total personal earnings.) Finally, a tax of 4 percent on personal incomes is levied to provide funds for the construction of housing. (Before 1961, the housing tax was 10 percent of wages and salaries; the lower tax has been made possible by reduced subsidies since rents were increased, as well as by recent increases in wages.)

Enterprises are also required to contribute 2 percent of their net incomes toward joint reserve funds for the benefit of enterprises, which are unable to earn adequate income because their equipment is obsolete or worn, because of unfavorable business conditions or for other reasons beyond their control (XIV). Communes are authorized to increase their contribution to 3 percent.

Beginning in 1961, enterprises also pay a tax equal to 20 percent of the part of net income which enterprises allocate to their operating and collective consumption funds (XV). Republics and communes will share in the proceeds of this tax equally and arrangements can be made for the districts also to receive some of the benefits.

Some enterprises must also pay federal turnover tax (VII), levied once in varying rates on the domestic sale of about 60 percent of all commodities. Once the most important instrument of policy and the greatest source of revenue, its primary purposes today are to capture excessive profits and to regulate consumption of commodities containing imported or otherwise scarce raw materials, commodities required for export, luxuries, or other articles (like alcoholic beverages and tobacco products), the consumption of which the Government wishes to restrict. The turnover tax rate varies from 5 to 60 percent and averages 10 to 15 percent. Communes, in agreement with their districts, are also authorized in some cases to levy a supplementary turnover tax averaging between 3 and 5 percent of selling prices.

Ricardian rent (VIII) must be paid by mines and petroleum companies which realize abnormally high profits on their output because of favorable conditions of operation, relative to other enterprises in the same branch of industry, or because they enjoy a monopoly position.

The balance remaining after deducting operating costs (II), turnover tax (VII) and Ricardian rent (VIII) from gross receipts (I) is called the "income of the enterprise" (IX). Prior to 1961, enterprise income was subject to a progressive tax, based on the relationship between income and the wage and salary bill of the enterprise. For most manufacturing enterprises no tax was payable on income up to 120 percent of the wage bill; thereafter the rate increased progressively when income exceeded 200 percent of the wage bill, when a tax of 70 percent was paid on the excess. However, if the ratio of income to the wage bill was higher than in the two preceding years, part of the tax was remitted to the enterprise as an inducement to increase profits. Beginning in 1961, the incomes of enterprises are generally subject to a flat federal tax of 15 percent (X). Construction enterprises (which work only seasonally) pay only 50 percent of the tax, while coal and nonferrous mines, coking plants, transport companies, agricultural cooperatives, food processing firms and enterprises in a variety of other branches are exempt from this tax. Newspapers and other publishing companies are also exempt from the tax, but republics may tax them up to 7.5 percent of their income to obtain resources for promoting publishing activity.

A temporary federal tax of 25 percent has also been levied on excess income earned by most enterprises (XI) in 1961. Excess income is defined as income allocated to enterprise funds which exceeds 6 percent of the aggregate value of the enterprise's working and fixed assets.

The financial allocations which the workers' council makes to its operating (or business) fund (XVIII) from its net income (XII), are used by the enterprise either as working assets, for the purchase of fixed assets or for the repayment of loans, the proceeds of which were used either as working assets or to purchase fixed assets. In the past, funds for working assets were held separately from those for fixed assets. Restrictions on the transfer of funds from one of these funds to the other led to situations in which some enterprises overinvested in fixed assets and did not have enough working assets. The consolidation of the two funds permits the enterprise to use the financial resources in its operational fund with greater freedom for either working or fixed assets, as required. Resources allocated from net income to the enterprise fund for collective consumption (XIX) are used by an enterprise to finance construction of housing, for improving the social welfare of workers and employees, scholarships, technical training and cultural and education activities.

The taxes and contributions described above are obligations of economic organizations and workers in the socialized sectors. A turnover tax, similar to the one payable by public enterprises, must be paid in the private sector by craftsmen on the sale of their products, by professional people on the sale of services and by sellers of real estate; there is also an employment tax of 5 percent. An income tax, consisting of a base tax and a progressive surtax, is levied on craftsmen, physicians, house owners and others in the private sector. There are also inheritance and gift taxes designed to limit the expansion of private property. Private farmers pay a tax which averages 16 to 17 percent of the cadastral value of their land (with the abolition of the land tax in socialized sector in 1961, socialized agriculture pays only income taxes). Compared with the socialized industry, which pays about one-third of its income in profit and wage taxes, the tax burden on private agriculture is light and partly offsets the effect of price policies which discriminate against agriculture; however, since price policy diverts income from private agriculture to socialized industry, there is less need to syphon off income from private farmers through taxation.

BIBLIOGRAPHY

A. BOOKS AND PAMPHLETS

"Abstract of Laws of the Federal People's Republic of Yugoslavia," in *Lawyers Directory*, 76th Edition, Charlottesville, Va., Lawyers Directory Publishers, 1958. pp. 2037-2066.

Auty, Phillis. *Building a New Yugoslavia*. London, Fabian Publications, 1954. pp. 29. (Fabian Society, London. Research Series, No. 165.)

Bicanic, Rudolf. "Interaction of Macro and Micro-Economic Decisions in Yugoslavia, 1954-1957," in Grossman, Gregory, ed. *Value and Plan; Economic Calculation and Organization in Eastern Europe*. Berkeley, University of California Press, 1960. pp. 346. (Russian and East European Studies.)

Bobrowski, C. *La Yugoslavie Socialiste*. Paris, Librairie A. Colin, 1956. pp. XVI, 273. (Fondation Nationale des Sciences Politiques, Paris, Cahiers 77).

Dragnich, Alex N. *Tito's Promised Land Yugoslavia*, New Brunswick, N.J., Rutgers University Press, 1954. pp. 337.

Free Europe Committee. Mid-European Studies Center. *Yugoslavia*. New York, Praeger, 1957. pp. XIII, 488.

Gerskovic, Leon. *Social and Economic System in Yugoslavia*. Beograd, Jugoslavija, 1959. pp. 97.

Korbel, Josef. *Tito's Communism*. Denver, University of Denver Press, 1951. pp. 368.

Kubovic, Branko, et alii. *Economic Planning in Yugoslavia*. Beograd, Jugoslavia, 1959. pp. 681.

Kubovic, B., and Trikovic, V. *National and Regional Planning in Yugoslavia*. Federal Planning Bureau. Beograd, 1961. pp. 48 plus three charts and maps. This article is also included as Chapter 6 in *Regional Economic Planning*, Walter Isard, Ed., published by the European Productivity Agency of the Organization for European Economic Cooperation, July 1961.

Lukic, Radomir. *The State Organization of Yugoslavia*. Beograd, Publicity and Publishing Enterprise, 1955. pp. 54.

McVicker, Charles P. *Titoism; Pattern for International Communism*. New York, St. Martin's Press, 1957. pp. XXI, 332.

106

Neal, Fred Warner. *Certain Aspects of the New Reforms in Yugoslavia.* Boulder, University of Colorado Press, 1953. pp. 53. (University of Colorado Studies. Series in Political Science, 1.).

Neal, Fred Warner. *Titoism in Action; The Reforms in Yugoslavia after 1948.* Berkeley, University of California Press, 1958. pp. XI, 331.

Neuberger, Egon. *Central Banking in Semi-Planned Economies: Yugoslav Case.* Unpublished Ph.D. thesis, Harvard University, Cambridge, Mass., 1957.

Nove, Alec and Donnelly, Desmond. *Trade with Communist Countries.* London, Published for the Institute of Economic Affairs by Hutchinson, 1960. pp. 183.

Papic, Augustin. *Investment in Economic Development in Yugoslavia, 1947-1956.* [Washington, EDI, IBRD] 1957. pp. 44 (Mimeographed). This article appeared in its original form in *Jugoslovenski Pregled* (Beograd), No. 9, 1957. pp. 423-434.

Papic, Augustin. *The Yugoslav Investment Bank.* [Washington, EDI, IBRD], 1957. pp. 13 (Mimeographed).

Sirotkovic, Jakov. *Novi Privredni Sistem FNRJ.* [New Economic System of the Federal People's Republic of Yugoslavia], Zagreb, 1954.

A Summary of the Draft of the Social Plan for Economic Development of Yugoslavia for the Period 1961 to 1965. Translation, mimeographed. pp. 28.

Teze o Nekim Pitanjima Privrednog Planiranja u Jugoslaviji. [Some Questions of Economic Planning in Yugoslavia]. Beograd, 1958. pp. 124 (Mimeographed).

Todorovic, Mijalko. *Current Problems of Economic Policy.* Beograd, Jugoslavija, 1959. pp. 55.

Sirotkovic, Jakov. *Problemi Privrednog Planiranja u Jugoslaviji:* [Problems of Economic Planning in Yugoslavia]. Naprijed. Beograd. 1961. pp. 413 (Mimeographed).

B. ARTICLES

Anjaria, J. J. "'The Economy of Yugoslavia," *India Quarterly* (New Delhi), Vol. 11, No. 4, October/December 1955. pp. 331-344.

Balog, Nikola. "The Status of Yugoslav Economic Enterprises," *The Eastern Economist* (New Delhi), Vol. 33, No. 8, August 21, 1959. pp. 279-280.

Baudin, Louis. "La Yougoslavie et le Communisme," *Kyklos* (Basle), Vol. 13, No. 3, 1960. pp. 327-345.

Bicanic, Rudolf. "La Concurrence Socialiste en Yougoslavie," *Economie Appliquée, Archives de l'Institut de Science Economique Appliquée* (Paris), Vol. 9, No. 3, July/September 1956. pp. 329-348.

Bicanic, Rudolf. "Economic Growth Under Centralized and Decentralized Planning: Yugoslavia—A Case Study," *Economic Development and Cultural Change* (Chicago), Vol. 6, No. 1, October 1957. pp. 63-74.

"Collective Economy in Yugoslavia," *Annals of Collective Economy; International Review* (Geneva), Vol. 30, No. 2/3, April/November 1959. pp. 105-363.

"Les Conseils Ouvriers Yougoslaves, II," *La Documentation Française, Notes et Etudes Documentaires* (Paris), No. 2629, February 15, 1960. pp. 1-24.

Davico, Jasa. "Communal Finance in Yugoslavia," *The Economic Weekly* (Bombay), Vol. 12, No. 19, May 7, 1960. pp. 705-707.

Djordjevic, Ivan. "Yugoslavia," *International Social Science Bulletin,* UNESCO (Paris), Vol. 8, No. 2, 1956. pp. 287-298.

Dupont C., and Keesing, F. A. G. "The Yugoslav Economic System and Instruments of Yugoslav Economic Policy: A Note," *Staff Papers,* International Monetary Fund (Washington), Vol. 8, No. 1, November 1960. pp. 77-84.

Horvat, Branko and Rascovic, Vlado. "Workers' Management in Yugoslavia: a Comment," *Journal of Political Economy* (Chicago), Vol. 67, No. 2, April 1959. pp. 194-198.

Mladek, J. V., et alii. "The Change in the Yugoslav Economic System," *Staff Papers,* International Monetary Fund (Washington), Vol. 2, No. 3, November 1952. pp. 407-438.

Montias, John Michael. "Economic Reform and Retreat in Yugoslavia," *Foreign Affairs* (New York), Vol. 37, No. 2, January 1959. pp. 293-305.

Neal, Fred Warner. "The Communist Party in Yugoslavia," *The American Political Science Review* (Washington), Vol. 51, No. 1, March 1957. pp. 88-111.

Neal, Fred Warner. "The Reforms in Yugoslavia," *The American Slavic and East European Review* (New York), Vol. 13, April 1954. pp. 227-244.

Neuberger, Egon. "The Yugoslav Investment Auctions," *The Quarterly Journal of Economics* (Cambridge, Mass.), Vol. 73, No. 1, February 1959. pp. 88-115.

"New Distribution of Income and Economic Enterprises." Translated from Privredni Pregled [Economic Review], (Beograd), March 6, 1961.

Petkovic, Miodrag. "Les Tendances Nouvelles du Developpement Economique en Yougoslavie," *Societe Belge d'Etudes et d'Expansion,* Bulletin Bimestriel (Liege), No. 175, March/April 1957. pp. 427-431.

Ray, P. K. "Economic Planning in Yugoslavia with Particular Reference to Agriculture," *The Economic Weekly,* July 1961. p. 1113.

Review of International Affairs (Beograd), Vol. 1, No. 1, 1950, and subsequent issues.

Stanovnik, Janez, "Planning Through the Market," *Foreign Affairs,* Vol. 40, No. 2, January 1960. pp. 252-263.

"The System of Investment and the Second Five-Year Plan of Yugoslavia," *AICC Economic Review* (New Delhi), Vol. 9, No. 14, November 15, 1957. pp. 28-30.

Ward, Benjamin, "Workers' Management in Yugoslavia," *The Journal of Political Economy,* Vol. LXV, No. 5, October 1957. pp. 373-386.

The Yugoslav Commune, in *International Social Science Journal* (UNESCO), Vol. 13, No. 3, 1961. pp. 379-448.

C. GOVERNMENT PUBLICATIONS

Yugoslavia. *Fundamental Law Pertaining to the Bases of the Social and Political Organization of the Federal People's Republic of Yugoslavia and of the Federal Organs of State Authority.* Beograd, Union of Jurists' Associations, 1953. pp. 99.

—————. *The Law on the Five-Year Plan for the Development of the National Economy of the Federative People's Republic of Yugoslavia in the Period from 1947 to 1951.* Beograd [Office of Information], 1947. pp. 166.

—————. *The Five-Year Plan of Economic Development of Yugoslavia, 1961-1965,* Federal Executive Council. Beograd, 1961. pp. 121.

—————. Economic Institute. *Privreda FNRJ—U Periodu od 1947-1956 Godine* [Economy of the FPRY, in the period from 1947-1956]. Beograd, 1957. pp. 396.

—————. Economic Institute. *Privreda FNRJ u 1957 Godini* [Economy of the FPRY in 1957]. Beograd, 1958. pp. 185.

—————. Federal Statistical Institute. *Index,* Monthly Review of Yugoslav Economic Statistics (Beograd), Year 8, No. 10, October 1959. pp. 56.

—————. Federal Statistical Institute. *Statistical Pocket-Book of Yugoslavia, 1960.* Beograd, 1960. pp. 257.

—————. Federal Statistical Institute. *Statistical Yearbook of the Federal People's Republic of Yugoslavia, 1959. English Text.* Beograd, 1959. pp. 231.

—————. Narodna Banka [National Bank]. *Annual Reports,* various [in English].

—————. Jugoslovenska Investiciona Banka. *Yugoslavia's Underdeveloped Regions (Conditions, Measures, Results and Possibilities of Economic Development).* Beograd, October 1961. pp. 20.